In the Field
with Horses

Praise for *In The Field with Horses*

"This delightfully profound book will help you discover what the ancients knew, and our civilization seems to have forgotten—how to literally tap into "horse sense" and "converse" with these wise and beautiful creatures. Even if you never come in contact with a horse, these stories alone will gently move you out of your head, and into your heart."

—Steve Bhaerman, co-author with Bruce Lipton of *Spontaneous Evolution: Our Positive Future* and *A Way to Get There from Here*

"Lisa Walters has written an inspiring book about navigating life with energetic awareness. In ten easy-to-read chapters, the reader is taken on a journey through relational and energetic concepts presented through the lens of connecting with horses. This book is a must-read for anyone curious about what can be learned through the way of the horse."

—Nina Ekholm Fry, MSSc., Director, Equine-assisted Mental Health, Prescott College

"In this beautifully written book, Lisa Walters describes how horses can teach us to live with increased awareness and presence, a feeling state which quiets the mind and brings forth peacefulness. If you love horses and are yearning to live a more creative and authentic life, this book will inspire you to do so!"

—Nancy Kersey, Licensed Marriage and Family Therapist

"In a clear and accessible way, Lisa Walters has provided a foundation for recognizing what is at the core of the human-horse relationship: energy, and how to understand it. Whether to illuminate your existing horse relationship, cultivate leadership qualities, or satisfy your sense that there is something more, this is timely wisdom that deserves to be shared."

—Tiffany MacNeil, Contributing Writer, www.HorseConscious.com and
Founder, Rocks and Rivers Outdoor Adventures

"Lisa explains several complex concepts in simple terms, bolstered by anecdotal stories from her own experiences. She is a gentle, effective teacher and her book will resonate in your heart. I plan on reading it many times to remind myself that the principles within need to be kept front and center in my life."

—Galen Miller, Venturing Awareness, Founder of Arabian Nights,
Dinner attraction, Orlando FL

"With deep respect, wisdom and insight, Lisa captures the dance between the human energy system and that of the equine. This book is a beautiful guide into that extraordinary realm."

—Constance Blake, Executive Leadership and Wellness Coach

In the Field
with Horses

Exploring the Horse-Human Connection

LISA WALTERS
founder of the EquuSatori Center

OVER AND ABOVE
PRESS

FIRST EDITION

Library of Congress Control Number: 2013918861

ISBN: 978-0-9890917-2-5

Design by Susan Shankin
Cover photo by Alycia Lang
Interior photos by Marianne Nishifue and Alycia Lang

For information, contact Over And Above Creative
18144 Killion Street, Unit 3, Tarzana, CA 91356.

Visit us at www.OverAndAboveCreative.com
Significant discounts for bulk sales are available.
Please contact: www.equusatori.com

Printed in the United States of America

Before me Peace, Behind me Peace, Under me Peaceful,

All around me Peaceful, — Peaceful voice when he neighs.

I am Everlasting and Peaceful.

I Stand for my Horse.

Navaho Song . . .

CONTENTS

ACKNOWLEDGMENTS

IT IS WITH APPRECIATION and gratitude that I would like to acknowledge the people who have played the key roles in my equine endeavors. First, I was fortunate to have loving parents who remained supportive even though they had no understanding of horses. I am grateful for their openness and the "long leash" they gave me that allowed me to find my own way.

It was Jim and Lois Walton who gave me my first horse. Jim not only saw an equestrian in me, he believed in and encouraged me. Jim started me on my initial path and continued his support by bringing me back to the Colorado mountains to ride for him in my mid-teens. During my summer riding for Jim, I gained a new level of self-confidence. This seeded my next chapter of showing and training horses.

Throughout my teens and early 20s, it was the entire Mitchell family, and in particular, Cathy, Lyda and Jane who were my (all things horse) family. The Mitchell family came into my life initially through friendship and then became so much more. They encouraged me, taught me, and hauled my horses to shows. The Mitchells supported me in too many ways to mention and I am forever grateful.

As I evolved in my understanding, it was my friend Marilyn Ferguson who initially encouraged me not to retreat from my own senses and to embrace the vision that was emerging. As I found the courage to stay out there, "on-the-limb," I found the wonderful, supportive and wise Barbara Rector, who shared my views and vision of the real potential in horse-human relations. Barbara has provided unending support, friendship, mentorship, and is a valued colleague.

I owe enormous gratitude to my husband Richard, who is the love of my life, best friend, and biggest source of encouragement. He has listened, edited, and inspired me to keep going forward. I also want to thank my daughter Alycia, whose very presence inspires me to be a better person.

Without the encouragement and professional guidance of Rick Benzel and Susan Shankin at Over and Above Press, this book may have never made it out of my barn and office.

Their skill and honesty are greatly appreciated and have played a key role in helping me with this project. In addition, Gayle Newhouse and William Gladstone (of Waterside Productions) provided just the right professional feedback and support at just the right time.

There is a large collective (I like to think of as my herd) of Equine Experiential Learning professionals and equestrians that I have connected with and befriended throughout the years. You all know who you are. I'm happy to say that the list is long and worldwide. I am grateful to have a connection with each of you. You are fellow torch bearers and together we have manifested a collective vision. While birthed in our individual hearts, we all share knowledge of the role horses play in the evolution of humankind. And our collective vision is now a reality that we can share with others. You are all visionaries and trail blazers. With appreciation and gratitude, I thank you all.

FOREWORD

THIS BOOK IS for any of us who has ever looked in a horse's eye and marveled at the reflected Mystery. Many of us may never own a horse or live in close proximity to those with horses, yet we've been inexorably curious and appreciative of the sight of horses galloping in a field or racing down a track at speed. Horses, we are learning, contribute to humanity's health and wellbeing.

In the Field with Horses goes well beyond the obvious reference to grassy paddocks where horses contentedly munch away their days or nights depending on your geographic location and horse stewarding practices. *Lisa speaks eloquently and knowledgeably of the Field of Energy that surrounds and connects all life.* She handily offers the practical principles horses teach us about this Field of Energy and how it works in our lives. Most importantly Lisa emphasizes the "how to" of reading horses. She decodes the "art of awareness"— paying attention in the present moment with a horse.

Readers are treated to practical steps in this account of Lisa's learning to work consciously with this field of awareness as she spent intentional time with her horses. These fields are measurably strong in horses and of powerful influence on humans. We now know that horses are affecting human's heart rate several minutes ahead of the human's influence on the horse. For people over fifty, their interaction with horses produces relaxation and elevated self-esteem. Regardless of age, one's immune system is enhanced.

Lisa has been instrumental in implementing many of the scientific studies examining the physiology of the horse and human relationship. Lisa's skill as a lifelong horsewoman complements her advanced studies in Energy and how it flows in our everyday lives. I find this an important and relevant topic for those of us caught up in a fast-paced quick-fix culture where the significance of Nature is increasingly being revealed as an important element of our mental, emotional, physical, and spiritual health.

I am delighted to know Lisa and call her friend, teacher, and colleague. I first met her when she traveled to Baxter Springs, KS to study with me and the Horses of Hope family in a five-day residential "Adventures in Awareness" (AIA) seminar exploring the invitational approach of AIA's equine facilitated experiential learning process work. I still remember the feeling of delight when greeting Lisa at the Joplin airport, warmed by her genuine smile and generous hug; I sensed I was meeting an old friend not yet known this lifetime.

It was soon apparent to me that this AIA student and now core teacher in the AIA Internship Program had a strong connection, understanding, and mastery of all things equine. I had located a kindred spirit who shared the classical model for schooling horses to their fullest potential, while also tuned to the role our inner landscape plays in the process.

Lisa knows horse as sentient being—guide, colleague, teacher, and co-creator in being fully present. What makes this work of Lisa's so compelling are her clear descriptive accounts of this awareness field as vibrant with energetic information, which horses, by their very instinctual nature, live in most of the time. Horses offer humans a connection, a relationship to an invisible realm of existence that most of us seldom think about, and upon which a horse's life completely depends.

The connection between humans and horses is the starting point that enables Lisa to connect her experiences with horses to the core gift they bring to mankind. Lisa weaves this gift with cutting-edge science, common sense skills and spiritual understanding in a profound refreshing and practical way.

Barbara K. Rector, MA, CEIP-ED
Adventures In Awareness, Founder & Director
www.adventuresinawareness.net
Skyview Casita, Tucson, AZ

PROLOGUE

———

Out beyond ideas of wrongdoing
and right-doing there is a field.
I'll meet you there.
When the soul lies down in that grass
The world is too full to talk about.

ᐤ RUMI ᐤ

RUMI SPEAKS OF "a field" that lies beyond our beliefs and judgments—a place that cannot be completely described by words. We all have experienced this place and we all have tried to depict it in the only way we can . . . with words. I believe this is the place we have all come from and the place that connects us to one another. It's a place beyond thinking, a place to be experienced.

Horses, too, graze in this field and if you join in relationship with them, having an open mind and heart, they will meet you there—and what you will learn will be life changing. Throughout my life, I have found myself in a state of presence with horses, sharing this peaceful space beyond belief and judgment. From this place, horses became my teachers, guiding my awareness to experience ever more subtle and beautiful ways that humans, animals, and all of nature are connected. The stories in this book relate what I experienced when I connected with horses in this field—and what those experiences subsequently taught me.

Eventually I coined a name for these "Ah-ha!" moments, calling each of them an EquuSatori—*Equus*, because they involve horses, and *Satori*, the Zen Buddhist term describing a "moment of enlightenment." This book is about the EquuSatories I experienced through my relationships with horses, and the insights I gained, which reveal truths about all relationships and life.

Horses are not solely beasts of burden, used for mere entertainment and sport. They are sentient beings whose unique gifts have benefited, and continue to benefit, the evolution of humankind. Much like we have dolphin encounters, people are now seeking out and appreciating equine encounters. Thanks to the many wonderful Equine Facilitated Experiential Learning (EFEL) or Equine Experiential Learning

(EEL) programs being offered throughout the world, practically anyone who wants to engage with horses can now do so. One no longer needs to own a horse or even ride a horse in order to learn from them.

When engaging with horses, it is important to know that they are masters at reading the *energetic field*. They are continuously responding to and interacting with what they sense and feel around them. When we learn to engage with them in this field, it enlivens our awareness of these abilities within ourselves. We not only experience more of ourselves but we also sense the influence we can have on our relationships. In having this type of *experiential learning*, we discover the wisdom we gain is not knowledge based solely in the head, but a much more integrated, holistic knowledge felt in our mind and in our heart. This knowledge is self-empowering.

Experiential learning is well accepted as the most integrated and complete form of gaining intelligence. When we experience something, it involves our physical, emotional, and intellectual bodies. Experiential learning provides more comprehensive and in-depth learning than a reading or viewing experience. In recent years, numerous Equine Experiential Learning programs have emerged around the world. People from all walks of life are engaging with horses, gaining self-awareness and self-empowerment skills with horses as their teachers. In an EEL program, the work is not therapy per se, but it is educational and often therapeutic. In an EEL program, there are no diagnoses or treatment plans like there are in Equine Assisted Therapy (EAP) or Equine Facilitated Psychotherapy (EFP) program. The horses are considered *colleagues* and are honored as sentient beings. Learning about and experiencing the specific qualities inherent in the horse's nature are the foundation for an EEL curriculum. From that learning, we gain self-knowledge and greater coherence within our own mind-body system. There is definitely a new awakening emerging with regard to our continual and ever-evolving relationship with the horse.

BEING IN THE FIELD

It was early in my life with horses that I realized my equine friends were modeling behaviors and honing relational skills in me that applied not only to my relationship with them, but to many areas of my life with humans. I noticed that whenever I was around horses I would settle into a peaceful state, and from there I'd have little (and sometimes big) realizations about situations or events I was going through. I also noticed that horses responded to me in a more positive and effective way when I was coming from this place of being with them. By learning to consciously step into this beingness—this place I refer to as *presence*—it seemed as if I could join them in a familiar and comfortable *field*. It felt to me that this presence is the "vibe" where horses engage, relate, and experience their own being. I also noticed that when I was in this state of presence, I too had more enlivened senses, resulting in an overall expanded awareness.

When working with horses in this presence, I believe we tune our awareness to a larger, more connected space where we somehow perceive reality with more than just our usual narrowed, modern, busy-life vision. Horses, in their essential nature—i.e., in what many of us in the EEL field call, *the way of the horse*—model life principles that can help us shift our perspectives, tap into our own creative sources, and connect more authentically with others. In understanding the horse's non-predatory and collaborative nature, we awaken a way to connect to more subtle and sometimes dormant parts of our own essence.

Horses have been human companions for millennia, perhaps since the dawn of *Homo sapiens*. In the most ancient cave drawings ever discovered, dating back as much as 30,000 years, horses were depicted as part of life. Without horses, human evolution would have no doubt taken a very different direction. Through our relationship with horses, we were able to expand our horizons. They enabled us to travel further and faster, helped us plow our fields, accompanied us through war, and today they continue to serve by inspiring us in a multitude of ways. The horse has certainly earned its noble status.

In cultures throughout the world, horses have long been considered revered companions, from the Celtic Epona, the loving horse goddess who protected all equines and represented fertility, re-birth, and abundance, to the prophet Mohammed's white horse "Barak," who carried him to heaven. History is filled with stories of horses that transported heroes bravely into battle, and were pioneers across distant lands and explorers into new worlds. This book is about the many ways in which horses also expand our awareness, carrying us to new perspectives and ultimately to further learning, growth and self-empowerment.

I consider horses a *gift to humankind*. When we engage with them, they invoke *presence* in us. They teach us how to listen with more than just our ears. Learning the way of the horse reveals keys that unlock our own subtle awareness and provides a path to connect us with our ultimate source of authentic leadership, power, and creativity. Unique to the process of interacting with a horse as "teacher" is the opportunity to learn and practice inter-relational skills in a non-judgmental space. Horses provide an *inner-active* experience, in which we learn to be fully engaged in a relationship by functioning in an expanded state of awareness.

Horses, like most animals, have a way of moving through their world in sync with nature. In general, they are relaxed, adaptable, and tend to remain in a calm state of beingness. Their ability to stay present enables them to tune in to a more heightened and expanded awareness, a skill they likely developed to help them survive in the wild.

When we join with horses in this peaceful, open field of presence, we become more physically and energetically attuned with them and we can more easily see and feel what's going on around and within *us*. What has been discovered in relatively recent scientific research (which measured indicators of this state of presence) is that when we shift into this state, the horse's energetic field tends to influence our own. We literally *join* them in this *field*. And when we consciously tune our awareness to this energetic field, our subtle sense perception expands, our perspective shifts, and we begin to experience and feel true connectedness. Heightened intuition and creativity occur in this state of being. By interacting with others from this centered and attuned internal place, we gain insight into the influence and power that our own intentions can have in relationships.

LEARNING COLLABORATION AND CONNECTION

As prey animals, horses have a clear social structure, as well as strict rules and boundaries within their herds. They can be very aggressive if need be, though their aggression is displayed primarily in setting boundaries. It is almost never used to actually harm another horse. The vast majority of their time is spent in a coherent, peaceful state where they *read the field*. Horses have developed extraordinary skills for sensing and avoiding aggressive predatory energy. They demonstrate for us how, from a grounded state of being in the present moment, we can best read and sense what is in the field around us, both physically and energetically. As Linda Kohanov, author of *The Tao of Equus*, eloquently points out:

> *It is the non-predatory aspects of the horse's nature*
> *that compliment the higher nature of humans.*

Horses are always looking for and will follow a leader. They know which of their cohorts is best suited to look out for the entire herd. They are not necessarily led by the biggest, strongest or fastest horse. Rather, they identify their leaders by how consistently those particular horses (or humans) use their awareness and energy to guide the rest of the herd to resources and safety.

Horses are *connected* and *collaborative* creatures who create deep bonds with one another. Their safety and security comes from finding community and following an authentic leader. Each member of every herd has a role and horses ultimately define their roles in *relationship* to one another. Like people, horses build lifelong bonds founded on trust and connectedness.

This place of equine connectedness is not unfamiliar to humans and the explanation for it is not mechanistic. The best way to understand and come to know this connection is to experience it. It cannot be known solely in the mind. It is perceived largely in the heart and sensed in our bodies. For me, it feels like an expansive, energetic, warm web that envelops us all, connecting us to one another. While it is always there, it is still and quiet, and so it is easy for it to fade into the background of our awareness. In a sense, it *is* the background of our awareness.

When we consciously bring our awareness to it through a *feeling* sense, we see that this place of connectedness is really a super-conductor of energy and information. In this state of presence, our physiology shifts toward *coherence* (where our brain waves literally become more in phase with the heart) and our intention has a much more direct influence on our actions. Our cortisol levels go down and all the "good hormones" that support health and healing increase. We are in what is commonly referred to as a *state of flow*.

Horses appear to reflect human feelings, often responding in kind to the energetic elements they perceive in their field of awareness. This phenomenon, inherent in a horse's nature, provides an amazing source of honest and instant feedback for those humans who intentionally and mindfully engage with a horse. This "mirroring" effect is a powerful communication tool. I suspect this ability was developed in the horse in order to help keep the herd resonating with one another and networked—demonstrating their connectedness as a coherent and congruent group. Perhaps this "merging energetically" is a way of getting to know others, to perceive what the other sees, to feel what the other feels, from their point of view. This is the ultimate empathy.

If we adopt the premise that horses can teach us that we are all connected and interrelated, we can begin to shift our thinking about relationships away from that based solely on individualism and autonomy. Our interest in others becomes less about what they can do for us to further our own agenda. Instead, *in the way of the horse,* we become willing to take on a sincere curiosity about others in order to discover who they really are and what they contribute to the whole. We become open to seeing and understanding how all of us fit into that whole, which also includes each person, their ideas, their individuality, and their intentions. This broader approach to relationships is modeled by horses within their herds. By joining with them, in this way of being, we can better appreciate the gifts that each and every human brings to the world, as well as learn to respect the interrelatedness of all beings.

SCIENCE CONFIRMS IT

This holistic state of presence and interconnectedness is supported by recent scientific research and discoveries. Quantum physics and string theory have revealed what science calls the *Zero Point Field*—in essence, an invisible energy field that connects and enlivens everything on this planet. Even our physical environment and climate reflect our interconnectedness. Throughout this book I will discuss elements of this scientific research that validates what horses, and other creatures, demonstrate for us.

As we gain a broader understanding about how *connected* everything in our world really is, it is time to begin shifting our collective paradigm. Now more than ever before, humankind is realizing that we do not live and work autonomously—and we can no longer afford to think and act as if we can. Within our local villages, towns, and cities, we see how we are a single global community. This causes us to shift our focus from the unique "I" (which is mainly concerned with "me") to a greater awareness about how "I" fits together with "we."

Horses help us *re-member* our true nature. They are masters in the *wisdom of we.* They awaken our senses and hone our relational skills and help us see the power of intention and relationship.

My understanding of these magnificent animals grew even deeper and broader when I was able to allow my own horses to live together in herds. In the herd setting, I witnessed how they interact with each other. I saw how horses individually evolved within the herd dynamics (in relationship to one another), and how they developed as leaders while also playing support roles to keep the herd together. It was not a far stretch to see how their relational skills apply to all relationships, including human ones. There truly is something about the nature of the horse that is good for the soul of humankind. They are mythical and archetypal to us, in part, because they always have been, and continue to be, willing allies in our noble pursuit of self-awareness and self-empowerment.

Horses provide an opportunity for all of us to acknowledge our interconnectedness and understand our direct influence on relationships. They help us find our own authentic leadership qualities and teach us to approach each moment with an open mind and heart—allowing creativity to flow. What follows in this book are true stories of my interactions with my own horses and the subsequent *EquuSatories* I gleaned from being with them. The insights modeled in these stories have helped me bring my awareness back to the magical field that connects all life. I have written these stories to offer you, as much as possible, the same "Ah-ha" moments I experienced.

ONE

Intent Has Infinite Organizing Power

—————

"You are what your deepest desire is.
As is your desire, so is your intention.
As is your intention, so is your will.
As is your will, so is your deed.
As is your deed, so is your destiny."

⌐UPANISHADS⌐

W E HAVE ALL had extraordinary and synchronistic things happen in our lives. And I'm sure we all wonder not only what causes them, but if it's possible to tap into some *zone* where more of them can occur.

Current scientific discoveries have begun to provide explanations for how synchronicity happens. First, contrary to what most of us have been taught, nature is not solely propelled by the survival of the fittest. Nature evolves more through the forces of cooperation than through competition. There is a larger connective field, a bigger picture, that we are all part of and continually interacting with. Our desires and intentions guide us by shaping our perception and awareness of things within the context of this *field of all possibility*. It turns out that *the nature of Nature* is an *optimizing force*, always looking for elegant, win-win opportunities. In effect, nature seeks balance, harmony, and optimization through connection and cooperation.

When I was nine years old, I wanted to go to summer camp, but only my brothers could attend that summer. My mother counseled me to *not resist* this unexpected detour from my long-awaited camp experience, but rather to open my mind to the possibility that something better (more optimal) could be lining up for me. As it happened, that summer I would deepen my understanding of what my mother was telling me about synchronicity and resistance through my first interactions with horses.

There is an ancient Sanskrit saying, *San Kalpa,* which means, as translated by Deepak Chopra,

> *My intentions have infinite organizing power.*
> *Intent weaves the tapestry of the universe.*

❧❧❧❧❧

Nature is an optimizing force, seeking confluence and win-win opportunities to orchestrate its ultimate plan of balance and harmony.

MAMA

Where it all started for me....

Horses appear to many of us as an archetypal presence; for me, they manifested first as a fascination and grew into an obsession. Evidently, I was *in the field* with horses before I even met one.

I'm not sure where my fascination with horses came from, but I know I was born with it. It didn't come from outside me. For the first seven years of my life, I lived where there were no horses. And no one in my immediate family shared my interest. Yet my favorite childhood game to play was "horses." I have memories of being three or four years old and wearing a dish rag tucked into my pants as a tail. I crawled around on all fours, imagining myself as a horse. Even though I had not yet spent any time with real horses, I was convinced that I had a memory of their smell and their sounds.

Later, when I had the good fortune to get a whiff of a *real* horse, it would send me into an altered state, prompting daydreams of horses in fields, complete with hay-filled barns, grassy fields, and worn wooden fences. Imagine my surprise when as an adult I discovered that the Sanskrit word *ashwagandha,* which is the name of a healing herb, means "the smell of a horse," implying that the smell of a horse actually has healing properties.

When I was seven, our family moved from northern California to Scottsdale, Arizona. There was still a bit of the "Wild West" in Scottsdale at that time. Best of all, there were *actual horses* to be seen all around. There were ranches, local horse shows, and occasionally I would see horses strolling with their riders down dirt paths that would become Scottsdale's busy thoroughfares in years to come. All these things gave me hope that real horses would one day be part of my life.

Finally when I was nine, I thought my time had finally come. It was summer break and my parents planned to send me, with my two brothers, to a swanky kids' resort in the Colorado Mountains for three weeks. This would give our parents some "alone time" and they planned to spend those weeks camping on private property at the base of beautiful Mount Columbia, not far from the kids' summer camp. I was beyond thrilled with this idea—I'd finally get to ride a real horse every day for three weeks!

Our plan took a big U-turn when a letter arrived in the mail stating that my brothers were accepted into their summer session but, unfortunately, the girls' camp was full! This news felt like a punch in my gut. I couldn't believe this was happening. I had been so invested in the plan that I had already been dreaming of the precise horse I'd be riding. I begged my mother to call the camp to see if there was any way they could swing it. How could they not make room for just one more kid? I told my mother to tell them that I was even willing to sleep in a pup tent if they just would let me attend.

I spent hours crying alone in my room; then my mother came in, sat on the bed, and tried to comfort me. She explained that it wouldn't be so bad, camping with Mom and Dad, without "the boys." But even this scenario didn't cheer me up. Mom added "one more thing" for me to think about, which did not make sense at the time, but would later spawn one of my biggest life lessons. She said, *"We don't always know what is in store for us. Sometimes when one thing doesn't work out, it's because something better is being lined up."* I remember correcting her that camping with Mom and Dad was NOT something better. And with that, I resolved to come to terms with my situation, sad as it was.

Summer finally arrived and our family began the trek from the Arizona desert up to the Colorado mountains. I beat back tears as we dropped my brothers off at what seemed like the most wonderful summer camp ever. I had to walk away with my parents.

The mountains in which we camped were truly beautiful, and the clear, clean air helped soothe and distract me from my emotional pain. We set up our camp trailer next to a stream at the edge of the forest where we could smell the fresh pine trees. With each breath, it felt as if we were joining with nature. There were miles of green grass on the valley floor spread out before us. Most mornings, before sunrise, the meadow would fill with a large herd of elk. They would graze until the sun fully rose, then silently amble back up into the forest out of sight. The land was clean and the atmosphere seemed magical. We could drink from the crystal clear, ice-cold stream and catch fresh rainbow trout in the pond near our campsite.

Our family friends, Jim and his wife Lois, were the owners of the land we were camping on. It so happened that Jim was an accomplished and lifelong horseman. We visited them every day, and in the evenings Jim often shared stories of his life in the U.S. Cavalry and his time training racehorses for Bing Crosby. Jim was a very tall man—he could have been John Wayne's twin brother. He was passionate about horses and I secretly envied that. I loved his stories and hoped that someday I could have horse stories of my own.

One afternoon, Jim turned to me and asked "Do you like horses?" His question spun me around. "Yes!" I shrieked, "I *love* horses." He continued, "Well, I have an old horse that lives here, up in the mountains. Sometimes if I call her, she will come down to visit. Would you like to come with me while I call her down and feed her?" Of course, this was a most exciting development and completely unexpected. Needless to say, I signed right up!

Jim, my father, and I walked to the edge of the woods where Jim began to call, "Mama! Mama!" He would wait a bit, blow a bullhorn, and then call her name again. We waited and waited for what seemed like an eternity. After a while, my heart began to sink; it looked like Mama was not going to come that day.

Suddenly, we heard the crackling of branches and the thunder of hooves, as a large buckskin quarter horse mare came galloping out of the forest. Mama was confident and eager to greet us. After we said our hellos, Jim fed her some grain. We brushed Mama's smooth coat. Jim looked over and asked me if I would like to ride her. I thought I would faint, this was so unexpected. I was excited, eager, and scared at the same time. I had only been on a couple of dude horses in the past and I wasn't sure I could handle a "real" horse. But an inner voice overrode my fears and I piped up with a definite "Yes!"

Jim put a bridle on Mama and lifted me, heart pounding, onto her bare back. Concurrently he was telling my father that other kids had tried to ride her before, but they usually couldn't get very far, because she just wouldn't do what they asked. His comments didn't make me feel very confident about what was about to happen. But now I was committed. At this point, I didn't even care if I rode anywhere; I was just overwhelmed with happiness that I was sitting on a real horse in these beautiful mountains. What more could a girl want?

I tuned out everything around me and immersed myself into the feeling of Mama's warm back and her magnificent smell. With a turn of the bridle and a little bump of my leg against Mama's side, we began to wander into the nearby meadow. As we meandered away, I would let her graze a while and then ask her to move on a bit. Then we'd stop to graze again. I'm not sure how I accomplished this, not having had any training, but somehow it worked out.

Eventually, I pointed Mama back toward Jim and my father, proud of the ease with which I had been able to direct her pace and destination. Jim turned and asked me, "Where did you learn to ride like that?" I had to be honest. "Nowhere. I never had any riding lessons." Jim asked me if I had done any practice riding back home. I replied that I had only been on horses once or twice, and they were dude horses at tourist ranches.

Jim stopped a moment to take in what I said, then turned to my father and remarked, "This is amazing. I haven't seen a kid with this kind of talent ever before." He went on to comment on my beautiful "natural seat" and my sensitivity in "working" with the horse. He told my father that if he had a kid with this type of talent, he'd make sure she got riding lessons. I could see that my father felt proud and happy for me. He didn't promise that day he would give me riding lessons, but it seemed like a start in the right direction.

The next day when we visited Jim and Lois, I asked if we could call Mama out of the woods again and Jim obliged. This time I got to blow the bullhorn. I called out, "Mama! Mama!" and pretty soon, I could hear the wonderful sound of hooves as Mama emerged from the forest. We continued to visit with Mama each day thereafter, and after about three days, she started to show up at our campsite on her own. I kept some carrots handy so I could entice her to keep coming back each day.

Mama's daily appearance was impressive to me because she was essentially living in the wild. She would have to roam a very long distance to even find a fence that might limit her travels. Mama had been living alone in the woods for a long time, though fortunately, during the winter, Jim turned one of his sheds into a shelter and supplemented her feed. Other than that, she was essentially allowed to wander freely and graze in the mountains to her heart's content.

What had seemed destined to be a long and boring camping trip with my parents had suddenly gone by in a flash. A few days before we were scheduled to leave, Jim gathered us together. He wanted to make a proposal. He explained to my parents once again that he thought he saw extraordinary potential in me as an equestrian. He understood that buying a horse was an expensive proposition and he could imagine it would be even more daunting if one didn't know much about horses. Then Jim got around to his point—he wanted to give Mama to me, as a gift! He saw a potential win-win opportunity if my parents said yes. He felt that the winters in the Colorado wilderness were hard on Mama. She was an older mare and would do much better in the warm desert of Arizona for her remaining years. And I seemed to get along beautifully with her. Jim offered to deliver Mama to me in Arizona, before winter and free of charge. He asked my parents if, under these conditions, they would allow me to accept this gift. Upon hearing this completely unexpected offer from Jim, I was so excited I could hardly think. My parents seemed to be receiving an offer they couldn't refuse. Something truly magical had just happened and I got to go home that summer knowing that by wintertime I would have my first horse.

My mother had been right—if I had gone to summer camp with my brothers, I would not have had this amazing opportunity. Something better than camp had actually lined up for me. It happened in a way and for a reason I could not fully grasp, but it was obviously real. Were it not for the synchronistic events that summer, my parents would likely not have discovered my potential as an equestrian. It took a twist of fate and a trusted family friend to point it out to them. I also appreciated the words of an expert who planted a seed of confidence in me—confidence that I could develop into a real equestrian. Until then, all I had were little girl dreams and a raw intention to create a deep connection with horses somehow in my life.

Mama was to be my first horse, the equine *mother* of my budding life with horses. It wasn't until many years later that I would fully understand what a perfect first horse she was. The many hours I spent just hanging out with her were key to helping me create a true bond with her, as well as initiating in me the *feeling* of *being in the field* with a horse. It was energizing and calming at the same time, a feeling that inspired me with awe and wonder as I studied her every move and basked in the presence of Horse.

Over the years I spent countless hours with Mama. I only rode her for short periods, preferring to bask in a peaceful state with her, watching her every move, and caring for her in the most loving way, without an agenda. I simply observed and felt my way into a relationship with her. This was the perfect situation for a 10-year-old and a gentle old mare. Through this experience, I became *infused* with the nature of horses, learning everything I could from my first horse, Mama.

TWO

All of Life is Interconnected and Interrelating at Every Moment

⌇

When we try to pick anything out by itself,
we find it hitched to everything else in the universe.
⌇JOHN MUIR⌇

W E HAVE ALL had the experience of thinking about someone or having a hunch or insight about them, and suddenly they call or show up. And whenever we enter a new situation, we take a "read" on how it feels, assessing if it feels friendly or even reminiscent of a place we once knew.

Whether we are conscious of it or not, our bodies are constantly reading and responding to our environment on both physical and energetic levels. The information gathered is fed back to us in the form of feelings, emotions, sights, smells, hunches, and insights. It is said that only 10% of perception takes place in the brain, while the other 90% is perceived from the neck down as feelings, and hunches. The perceptions associated with the nervous systems related to our gut, heart, and other organs hold essential information regarding what's going on around us. We are essentially feeling for our interconnectedness.

We now suspect this to be true from new insights created by the sciences of quantum physics and string theory, and the discovery of mirror neurons inside our bodies. Thanks to new super-sensitive technologies, we can now describe and measure ever more elusive and subtle *realms of reality*. Scientists have identified what is called the Zero Point Field. This is the energetic web of life that connects and contains us all. This giant web is continuously communicating with all elements of its infinite self. Within this field, time is not only linear, it is instantaneous. Lynne McTaggart describes the Zero Point Field in her book *The Field*:

> *Dozens of scientists in prestigious areas around the world have demonstrated that all matter exists in a vast quantum web of connection and that an information transfer is constantly going on between living things and their environment. Still others have produced evidence suggesting*

that consciousness is a substance outside the confines of our body. The brain and DNA, always assumed to be the body's central conductors, should more properly be considered transducers — which transmit, receive from, and ultimately interpret quantum information picked up from the Field.

These discoveries raise the question: Is it possible to consciously "tune" ourselves or direct our own awareness in a way that we can interpret more information through this field? I believe the answer is yes and it's not as unfamiliar to us as we might think. Perhaps we have always been privy to more information from the energetic field around us, but we have tuned our dial to pick up only a narrowed scope of thought relating to our past, along with our fears projected onto a future that hasn't revealed itself yet. Lynn McTaggart writes:

Some scientists went as far as to suggest that all of our higher cognitive processes result from an interaction with the Zero Point Field. This kind of constant interaction might account for intuition or creativity — and how ideas come to us in bursts of insight, sometimes in fragments but often as a miraculous whole. An intuitive leap might simply be a sudden coalescence of coherence in The Field.

It is not only science that informs us of our interconnectedness. Thousands of years ago, the ancient Vedic text *Aham Brahmasmi*, also offered a description of this connection. In a translation from the Sanskrit, Deepak Chopra cites this passage:

> *The core of my being is the ultimate reality, the root and ground of the universe, the source of all that exists . . . . Awareness of this silent witness is the beginning of awareness of the conscious intelligence field — the source of all the synchronicities in our lives . . . . Imagine that the whole universe is being played out inside you. Imagine that you are connected to everything that exists.*

THE GIFT OF DIORA
Connecting through the "Field"

Perhaps you've noticed that we seem to attract certain people into our lives who provide particular gifts and lessons we need at that time. This becomes evident to us as we engage in relationship with them. We also attract horses who seem to have the precise gift for something we need. Just as people have certain talents of their own, each horse has a unique talent, too.

Diora was a spirited Arabian mare given to me as a wedding gift. When I received her, she was a beautiful two-year-old filly, playing in the pasture and regularly getting into mischief. One of the first unique things I learned about Diora was that she liked to eat unusual foods. Her strangest craving was orange peels. If I brought an orange to the barn and peeled it in front of her, she would drop everything, stare at the peel and do everything short of snatch it out of my hand in order to have it. This was her all-time favorite treat, unusual for a horse.

In her youth, Diora competed in halter classes—beauty and conformation contests—at horse shows. She won "Champion" or "Reserve Champion" mare at every show she attended. As she matured and it came time to prepare her for riding, the process was easy and gentle. When she was about five years old, I started asking her to work with me in the arena for longer periods. It was at this time, asking her for a little more focus and effort in her work, that I noticed her preference for the trail over the arena. She was willing to work in the arena but didn't seem as happy as when we were out in nature. Despite this, I gently persisted with her arena training, believing she needed to learn more of the conventional basics in order to prepare for carrying the weight of a rider so she could have a healthy career under saddle.

Right from the start, Diora showed signs of being a very sensitive and communicative horse. While temporarily boarding her at a facility with lots of other horses and trainers, I noticed she was getting depressed. The light in her eyes seemed dimmer when I'd come to greet her. And often she'd be standing with her head in the corner of her stall looking sad. In addition, she didn't seem eager to come out into the barn area. I began to question why this might be, only to discover there was a very angry (and I would even say *cruel*) trainer brutalizing horses under his care. All the people in the barn were disturbed by this. When I became aware of this negativity in her life, I moved Diora to a friend's house. She perked right up, becoming her happy self again. She quickly became bright-eyed and enthusiastic

You'll see it when you believe it.
WAYNE W DYER

again. Diora's sensitivity and clear communication skills were uncanny. After that incident I had a newfound respect for her and started paying even closer attention to her actions, with more curiosity. I began what I eventually would call "listening with awareness."

As time went on, whenever I worked in the arena with Diora instead of on the trails, I kept having the recurring thought that I shouldn't be training her there. I would shove this thought back out of consideration each time, countering it again and again with my belief that basic classical dressage training had to be done in an arena. But my subtle inner feeling that something was amiss persisted, contrary to my beliefs.

One day, (seemingly) unrelated to anything to do with my horses, friends called to share a story about an interesting experience they had. They claimed to have had a very "insightful" phone conversation with a group in Canada called Trillium. They suggested my husband and I should try talking to them as well. Trillium was supposedly a "channeled" group of entities, available for special consultation with individuals. I wasn't sure what that meant, but out of respect for our friends, I stayed open and curious. Having a "session" with them seemed like a weird thing to do. We didn't think we believed in channeling, but what was the harm? I welcomed it as a fun adventure.

Shortly after my conversation began with the Trillium group, the voice on the phone said to me, "We are glad that you have made yourself available through the love of horses. This is not your first lifetime with horses. You had a lifetime in England where you bred Arabian horses." At this point, they had my attention. They had no way of knowing I was involved with horses and equally perplexing was the fact that Diora was an English Crabbett-bred Arabian.

They—that is, the group represented by the one voice—proceeded to say, "There is a horse that you have now that would like to give you a message. The message is that 'she would like you to stop the structure.' That is to say, the way you are being with her . . . or the activities you currently do together."

By now I was floored. How did they know I had a horse or even that it was a female? And of course, I had been having these recurring thoughts and feelings about where and how to continue Diora's training. Our talk went on as they told me a few other things . . . but I only remembered the message from the horse. Needless to say, I clearly got the point.

After reconciling the phone conversation with my own recurring thoughts, I finally concluded that Diora had to engage with me in her way. I would have to make a radical change to my approach with this horse. I would have to *stop the struggle,* which was directly proportional to my own attachment to my single-minded beliefs about horse training. Diora had been trying to tell me this but my beliefs kept me from listening. The unconvential communication from the Trillium group certainly had gotten my attention and I learned my lesson. I decided to "accept what is" and go with the flow.

That evening my husband and I walked out to the barn to tell Diora. When we arrived, I found her lying down in her stall. She didn't raise her head as she normally did to greet us. I got closer and spoke to her; I could see by the look on her face that she was awake and peaceful. She had the softest eyes that seemed to be inviting me to come closer. I knelt down by her head and told her that I got the message and was going to "let go of the structure." I declared that she was free to be whoever she was and I would love her just the same. After my declaration, Diora raised her head and nuzzled me; then she put her head in my lap and let out a big sigh. She continued to moan and sigh. It felt like she and I were letting go of mountains of stress. She was clearly in a state of bliss. She allowed me to hug and rub her as she moaned and yawned for the longest time.

That day marked a new beginning on my journey with Diora. I had no idea of the direction we were going in her training, yet there was something very freeing about that.

Our relationship changed from me being "the one who knows" to the two of us being "colleagues." We were both teacher and student. Diora and I had connected, somehow, through this most unusual channel.

Through the Trillium group, Diora and I were evidently plugged into some unifying field. Of course, I was left with many questions: How could the voice on the phone know all this about my horse and me? Were they reading and responding to some mysterious energetic field of information I was emitting? Was it possible that they received this information from both Diora and me? Whatever the method of communication was, it wasn't in my normal toolkit. I was left with a more curious open mind and heart, ready to embark on a wonder-filled new beginning.

THREE

The Keys to Connecting . . .
Presence and Awareness

You cannot be present in an abstract way.
Presence is not about disappearing into nothingness.
You can only be present with something
that is actually here.
—LEONARD JACOBSON—

*In presence,
our subtle awareness
expands, we experience
the "gentle presence"
that holds the whole
of everything without
judgment — equally.*

IN A STATE of presence, we begin to sense and experience the connectedness of life around us. We are more in tune with subtlety within our field of awareness; the world becomes more charming—the mind quiets. With fewer thoughts, judgment is replaced with discerning. There, we join in a palpable backdrop of peace and connectedness. There, life seems to unfold with a certain grace, at the directive and pace of inner guidance. Presence is not a mental state, it is a feeling state.

In the book entitled *Presence*, Peter Senge, C. Otto Scharmer, Joseph Jaworski and Betty Sue Flowers write:

We've come to believe that the core capacity needed to access the field of the future is presence. We first thought of presence as being fully conscious and aware in the present moment. Then we began to appreciate presence as deep listening, of being open beyond one's preconceptions and historical ways of making sense.

Presence is one of the primary keys to consciously entering the field.

Presence has a direct link in opening the door of Awareness and beginning what I like to call *authentic connection*. Presence and Awareness enhance understanding in one's relationship to anyone (or anything). Presence and Awareness are intricately connected; in fact, they are two sides of the same coin. It is hard to determine which comes first, as both are passageways to one another and always lead to an awareness of ever-more subtle realms of reality. By allowing our thoughts to drift away from habitual loops, we can create the space to perceive something new.

Shifting toward a place of connectedness need not be a struggle. It is a matter of loosening our grip or attachment to current thoughts and feelings. It's allowing ourselves to explore, to be curious and imaginative. Being in a space of connectedness is not unfamiliar to us and the explanation for shifting toward Presence is not mechanistic. Presence is simply an experience. It cannot be known solely in the mind; it is felt, largely in the heart. It is still, deep, and all encompassing.

When we consciously bring our awareness to the present, through a *feeling* sense, we experience a super-conductor

In a state of true presence, we become more aware of the connectedness and relationship of all life, communication is effortless and direct.

of energy and information influencing our awareness and attention. In a state of presence, intention has a more direct influence.

Horses reflect or mirror energy, often responding in kind to the energetics they perceive in their field of awareness. This is what I call authentic empathy. A horse is feeling, sensing, smelling, hearing, and seeing what is in their field at all times.

Imagine that the horse is generating a peaceful coherent bubble (a state of presence) around itself while interconnecting and grazing with its herd mates. When any one horse in the herd becomes startled, a ripple of fear (a disturbance in the field) is perceived by all. Every horse immediately feels this disturbance and will react in kind. A startled horse doesn't take the time to consider if the fear he perceives is from himself or another in the herd; he simply responds appropriately to what he perceives as fear energy. If he took the time to think it through, he would lose precious seconds and possibly suffer an attack by a predator. This is one of the ways horses communicate with one another; by example, they can get others to look around also. This type of awareness is an effective communication tool and survival mechanism. By being continuously connected energetically to subtlety in their field of awareness, horses stay in synchrony with the energy of the entire herd. This is how they keep in touch.

It is often said that a horse knows when you are afraid. This is because when a fearful person comes into a horse's space, the same thing happens—the horse perceives the fear and may start looking around to see what there is to be fearful of, behaving with concern and mirroring the human's energy of concern.

DIORA READS THE FIELD
Insights on empathy and telepathy

As I embarked on my new beginning with Diora, I found myself spending time with her largely as I did with my first horse, Mama—without an agenda. I became increasingly curious and aware of the subtleties in our relationship. By responding to her in kind with more subtlety, a deeper connection began to emerge between us. In time, I would realize that this deeper connection was not just unique to her; it is available with all horses. As each nuance of communication revealed itself with Diora, I gained a greater sense of awe and wonder and wanted to explore even more.

We began spending time either on trail rides in the desert or simply interacting during grooming and barn chores. On occasion I would lunge her in the arena (in lunging, the horse moves around the handler with a long line attached to the halter). One day while lunging her, I started to notice that she was changing to the next gait a second or so before I would ask her to do so with my verbal command. I issued a gentle correction and told her to wait until I verbally asked her to change gaits. I thought I was asking her to listen to me more carefully and I interpreted her jump-the-gun behavior as making decisions on her own.

Then I had a little hey-wait-a-minute thought, a sudden insight: "How is she figuring out what I am going to say, before I even say it?" After all, she was consistently changing into the correct gait—just not when I verbally asked for it. At first, I thought I must have been giving her subtle body cues or perhaps I was following a consistent pattern she had memorized. So, I purposefully stood stock-still and radically changed the patterns and eliminated any physical cues. Still she kept changing gaits before I verbalized my request. I further mixed up my requests and made sure I wasn't clicking, blinking, or even licking my lips before I asked her to change gaits. Sure enough, she still made the correct gait changes before I asked.

By this point, I was fully engaged with curiosity and a sense of play. I further experimented. I began not saying anything at all, just thinking about which gait I wanted her to move into. Sure enough, she would respond accordingly at the moment I had the thought. I asked without any words that she move from walk to trot and then to canter, a pretty standard pattern for me. But then I switched it up and asked by only thinking and feeling the rhythm of each gait. Together we went from trot to walk to halt and then canter. By this time I was really having fun, testing and retesting this new way of communicating with her. My bafflement was growing and I kept wondering what subtle cues she was picking up in order to know which gait to choose.

I reflected on what conditions were present within me and within Diora that might help explain the hows of this subtle interaction. There were a few factors that I thought of. First, both Diora and I were very present and hooked into each other. I was not thinking about anything else and my mind was still. I kept a questioning curiosity and a sense of objective observation, rather than rushing to a conclusion. Both of us were also relaxed, and we had a palpable connection that was calm and grounded. This led me to feel that perhaps we had created a sort of energetic bubble we were both enveloped in.

When you judge another, you do not define them, you define yourself.
WAYNE W DYER

In addition, every time I had a "thought request" for her, I coupled it with a conscious and distinct feeling or energy I got in my mind and body. For instance, "walk" felt to me like a focused four-beat march. Trot felt like a rhythmic two-beat dance, and canter felt like three beats of sheer delight. All my new subtle cues were congruent, meaning my thoughts, feelings, and intentions were all aligned. I wondered if I was transmitting the feeling of the gait I wanted to have her match.

It was clear that Diora was tuning in to something and I could only imagine it was a subtle energy field between us. She seemed to identify perfectly the feeling of each gait as I experienced it inside me. I started consciously and with intention working with this idea. I would feel the walk in my own body and I would picture her doing it.

Once I caught on to Diora's degree of energetic subtlety, I began to exhale silently whenever I asked for a downward transition. I transmitted to her the rhythm of the walk. I was being the walk before and during my verbally silent asking. The same was true for trot and canter. Once I identified the consistent feelings that corresponded to each gait, I would simply direct my focused feeling of that gait toward Diora's heart and sure enough, she would respond accordingly. I was literally being the change I wanted to see.

It felt as if I was sending energy messages to the center of her body. Was the horse's center, where the heart resides, the energetic central station rather than the head? Somehow, I intuitively felt that the most effective connection between us was from heart to heart. It wouldn't be until years later that I would discover the truth of this—that the nervous system related to the heart does actually perceive and respond to electromagnetic fields seconds before the brain. It seems we all partake in this type of telepathic form of communication (tele- meaning transmitting and -pathic as in empathy or shared feeling). We are normally so focused on audible and visual cues that we aren't aware of the energetic component attached to the transmissions we send and receive in our feeling body.

I decided to put my theory to the ultimate test. If Diora was really listening to my energy, my telepathic cues, then the lunge line wouldn't be necessary. So I unhooked it, leaving Diora free to walk away if she pleased. Then I consciously kept generating the same feeling between us as if nothing had changed and I fully expected she would stay and play. I asked her again non-verbally to go through her paces. She did exactly as I asked, when I asked.

When you change the way you look at things, the things you look at change.
WAYNE W DYER

After practicing this for a few minutes, I could see that the more congruent and subtle my instructions were, the more effective my intentions and directives became. I had awakened to a whole new dimension of communication with my horse. At this point I was very impressed and I felt I had gained consistency and confidence in my new mode of communication, so I called for my husband to come out to take a look at what was going on. He stood by the arena, quietly watching while Diora and I went through the paces. We halted, reversed, and did all three gaits in the opposite direction, all without a lunge line. When we finished, I said to him: "Well, what do you think?" He replied, "About what?" I replied, "About Diora going around like that with no line and no verbal commands." To this, he replied, "I thought that was what you always did."

At first I thought that this showed that what I was doing wasn't particularly impressive to my husband. But then I realized that perhaps he was right: I had always been doing this, but I had not been consciously aware of it and I therefore did not consciously work with it as a tool.

Although I didn't know how the rest of the world would describe this type of communication, I decided to name it telepathic communication. In this case, the idea that such telepathic communication could exist didn't seem so "out there" to me. It seemed quite practical and simple. I was clearly influencing the relationship between Diora and me via the energetic field between us. And I was doing this with the subtlest of cues, starting with Presence and Awareness. I now saw the influence of intention in my relationship with Diora. She was right there with me, accurately interpreting this most subtle form of information.

I wondered if this level of communication is all it takes to get the job done; perhaps my former style of talking, clicking, and popping the lunge wand seemed like shouting to the horses. At the very least, those other ways were no longer my only tools. I had discovered a much more interesting and empowering language—the combination of presence, awareness, energy, and intention.

Intention, combined with presence and awareness, points the way for manifestation.

Feelings are transmissions . . . expressions of Energy . . .

FOUR

Listing With Awareness

There is a voice that
does not use words . . . Listen.

✑RUMI✒

The horse stood on its hind legs . . . . I could smell it, so lovely . . . . I could hear it breathing, so exciting . . .

WILLIAM SAROYAN

ISTENING TO AUDITORY stimulation is only one way of listening. Sometimes we need to pay attention in a broader way. Normally when we listen, we are highly focused on only one thing—sound. When we *listen with awareness*, we expand our attention to include not only our outer environment but our inner landscape as well. In order to get a more holistic picture, we must listen to the physical, emotional, energetic, and environmental stimuli. We need to expand our awareness to be open to it all.

Fortunately, our body comes highly equipped to do this. It is an amazingly complex organism. My friend, mentor, and colleague Barbara Rector aptly calls it our "bio-suit." One of the abilities our body has is the ability to listen with awareness, which is found in our many different nervous systems. The gut has a nervous system and the actual heart organ has a nervous system as well. As mentioned in the previous chapter, we now know that the heart's nervous system directs organs to respond to what it perceives seconds before the brain is involved. In addition, science has revealed that we all have what are called mirror neurons, whose job is to pick up on the emotional states of others.

We spend most of our life focused on and aware of only our five physical senses, but by learning to listen with awareness; by tuning our awareness to more subtlety, our capacity to receive, perceive, and transmit more information can expand. We should all seriously consider the benefits of this type of expanded perception—a sensitivity that leads to more creativity and intuition. Many people have trouble believing in the existence of anything they can't see, hear, taste, smell, or touch. Yet we are all capable of so much more. In effect, we are created to perceive and interact with "the entire field" around us. When we tune or direct our awareness to ever-more layers of perceptions and subtleties, we can start to realize that we are not just the matter that makes up our body-mind physiology; we are also connected to the source that energizes, animates, and directs it. From this perspective, our bodies do occur more like a complex "bio-suit."

Expanding our sensitivity to include everything we can be aware of is listening with awareness. This enables us to make decisions and take action from a more informed place, utilizing more of our senses—perhaps activating our awareness of sensory input we didn't even know we had. Sometimes it is our "gut "instincts that direct us from harm's way. Sometimes situations just don't "feel" right or safe to us. These are our physiological responses to our environment, which help us pace and direct ourselves.

It is my conviction that the capacity for more subtle sense perception can be honed through our interactions with horses. Horses help us tune and train our abilities to perceive the subtleties around us and interpret what we take in. They can help people remember how to *read the field,* using additional perceptive awareness other than our usual default visual and verbally dominant sense organs. Perhaps not having developed the capacity for complex verbal language, horses have instead developed other ways of communicating and staying interconnected within their herd.

For me, the first door to unlock is the door of our beliefs. A useful set of givens, formed by our direct experience with in our families and our culture, our beliefs prompt in us a barrage of repeat thoughts. These repeat thoughts form deeply entrenched neuro-pathways in our brains. They become an automatic filter and lens, directing and influencing our perceptions. Beliefs can be appropriate when they are initially formed, yet become inappropriate if they do not evolve as we grow older and desire change in our lives. If we want to stay in the driver's seat of our own perceptions, we need to become aware of the anachronistic beliefs influencing us and be willing to loosen our grip on (our attachment to) them in order to perceive something new.

Judgments, stemming from our beliefs, have a big influence on our perceptions. Judgments are a form of already knowing. They do not contribute to an open-minded and expanded receptive or perceptive state. While horses are quick to learn habits, identify patterns, have excellent memories and discernment, they don't hold judgment the way

Listening with Presence echoes back the resonance of the person speaking . . .

humans do. Judgment narrows the field of our perception and this is the last thing a prey animal wants to do.

Judgment is very different from discernment. While judgment narrows perception, discernment helps direct and inform from a broader perspective, without attachment. When we are present, listening with awareness, and when we loosen our grip on our beliefs, judgment dissolves into discernment. We become more adaptable, nimble, more in touch with our intuition and creativity. Discernment rather than judgment is one quality that helps horses be so adaptable and responsive to their environment and field of awareness.

When we come to engage in relationship with horses with an attitude of play and exploration—having loosened our grip on our beliefs and judgments, bringing our awareness to the present moment, listening to the feedback of our bio-suits, the emotions, the thoughts, and the tingles of our nervous systems—we can begin to experience more forms of communication.

DIORA LEADS ME HOME

In Stillness . . . without agenda or fear . . .
we find direction

After months of spending time with Diora without a rigid agenda, I began to settle into a different rhythm with her. I found myself perceiving the barn and all the activities associated with being with her in a more holistic and magical way. I began considering how everything in my environment might be interacting with me and how it might be informing me of energies and messages I was not receiving. I started perceiving things differently and noticing subtleties that I had previously missed. I also started to see more coincidence and synchronicity in all areas of my life.

One warm sunny day, I went out to the barn to saddle up and go for a trail ride. As I calmly groomed Diora, my thoughts drifted. I was thinking about how long I had lived in the desert and how many stories I had heard of people coming across snakes. I felt grateful that I had not come in contact with any snakes, particularly rattlesnakes . . . as they seemed too scary to come upon while on a horse. I considered the possibility that one reason I hadn't seen any snakes was because I really didn't want to see them. Then I reconsidered and thought to myself, "If I saw a snake now, it would probably be O.K." I realized I could handle it.

We seem to be the only species of animal that gets "lost" in our own environment. We have all the necessary faculties, such as mental reason, creativity, and intuition; but in our culture it seems we are rarely taught how these faculties interact. As a result, we rarely consciously employ them or realize the real value of them.

I saddled up and headed out into my favorite desert washes and remote dirt roads for a nice ride. Diora and I started on our usual paths, admiring the huge saguaro cacti and ironwood trees alongside the trails. After a while, I veered off onto a wide dirt road that I thought I had gone down before. Diora and I did a good couple miles of trotting until we came to a crossroads that was unfamiliar to me. At this point, I realized I had gotten turned around and wasn't sure which way was home. When I first realized that I could actually be lost, I had a moment of panic. I was shocked at how quickly and easily I had gone off course. All the roads and washes were so similar, and the abundant desert trees were just tall enough that they blocked my view to locate where I was.

I had to force myself to sit still and consciously get my emotions calmed. I quieted my fearful thoughts by replacing them with clear reasoning. In a calmer, more centered state, I regained some degree of presence and remembered that Diora would always find her way home eventually. But worry again overcame me, and I considered trying to backtrack and find my way in reverse. The reverse plan seemed dicey though, because I hadn't paid attention to which way I had turned miles back.

So I sat at the proverbial crossroads for a time, waiting and trusting that inner guidance would indicate which way to turn. When I felt calm again, I decided that my best bet was to see which direction Diora would choose. Immediately upon my having that thought, she started to walk toward the road to the left. She stepped out with unusual confidence without my prompting, something she wouldn't normally do. Her taking the lead at this juncture felt right and comfortable. Not long after taking the left road, I heard a faint screech from a large parrot-like bird. I had heard this sound while riding out here before. It was a very unusual and noticeable sound in the desert. It must have been a caged bird, whose voice traveled a long way. I took it as a sign that we were close to familiar territory and heading in the right direction. The birdcall was so faint that if I had not been quiet inside and really listening to subtlety, I would probably not have noticed it.

Diora and I were trotting along at a good clip when all of a sudden I heard a voice in my head say "STOP." I did just that and as I came to a halt, the gold necklace I was wearing fell off from around my neck and landed directly in my hand. I proceeded to place my treasured necklace into the zippered pocket of my breeches, with a deep sense of gratitude for the inner voice that had brilliantly stopped me just in time. I patted Diora on the neck in an effort to share my gratitude. She and I stood still for a minute, feeling appreciation and gratitude for our inner guidance. I suddenly started to feel more connected to something bigger than myself. The coincidence seemed like validation and gave me a sense of peace, as well as one of awe and wonder.

When I refocused on the task of finding our way home, I looked up to find myself at yet another crossroads, only this time I clearly recognized where I was and I knew which way to go. What was remarkable about this was that if I had not been guided to stop at that exact spot, I could have trotted right past my correct path home. I was filled with a sense of gratitude and joy. And was deeply appreciative of this lesson in how to find self-confidence and presence in a fearful situation.

All the way back to the barn, I reviewed the magical, synchronistic events of this ride. This experience showed me how aligning with my inner stillness was a key to allowing me to take direction not only from Diora, but from the whole environment. I returned home with a full heart.

And if that wasn't enough, Diora and I approached the tack room at the barn only to find a huge king snake stretched out in the sun. This confirmed it for me: all I had to do was be open to the possibility of things, from seeing snakes, to being guided home . . . and the field of all possibility obliged.

FIVE

Subtle Awareness Expands Perception

~

"Quantum physicists had discovered a strange property
in the sub-atomic world called 'non-locality.'
This refers to the ability of a quantum entity such as
an individual electron, to influence another quantum
particle, instantaneously, over any distance,
despite there being no exchange of force or energy.
It suggested that quantum particles once in
contact retain a connection even when separated,
so that the actions of one will always influence
the other, no matter how far they get separated."

LYNNE McTAGGART,
The Field

If you listen with awareness, you will find that you hear in new ways and gain a new perspective.

A S WE HAVE SEEN, in the field, where we are all connected, in that open feeling place of love and compassion, free of our narrowed perceptions of judgment, we
discover new perspectives and gain knowledge. In a state
of presence, subtle awareness expands our perception.
As our perception expands, we become aware of a larger
shared field of being. We begin to realize that the transfer
of information comes in many different forms. With horses
(and other animals as well as humans), these communications include pictures and feelings. When we perceive
these transmissions, they can occur to us as instantaneous
impressions or intuitive knowing.

Consider that sometimes when you feel something, it
may not have originated with you and it may not be solely
about you. It may be a feeling, picture, or emotional impres-
sion generated and transmitted by someone else—and you
are simply perceiving it. When this happens in the presence
of a horse, it may be part of a conversation that the horse is
trying to have with you.

In presence, there is inner stillness and non-attachment. We perceive feelings and experience emotions without falling into the trap of identifying ourselves as the emotion itself. Instead of "I am frustrated," you might say, "I am feeling frustration." This is a more objective viewpoint; while at the same time it can help you fully experience what is going on inside and outside you in the moment. Everybody and everything emits energy (emotion = energy in motion). When we perceive energy, it is actually resonating with us. Whether it originates from within us or not, it has a corresponding feeling (the resonance), which we interpret as emotion.

From this perspective, emotional process becomes one of simply being present and curious about feelings, images and information, without judgment. And from this perspective, we gain a broader, more comprehensive interpretation of that of which we become aware. This is . . . *The way of the horse.*

In Bruce Lipton's book *Spontaneous Evolution*, he points out that the "thinking" part of our brain is much slower than the larger "processing" part. Most of what we perceive takes place in this faster, non-verbal part of our brain. What prevents us from listening to this non-verbal processing area and tuning in to the state of flow it creates is the noise in our mind. Neuroscience explains why this happens in our brain physiology. Our brain is constantly engaging in an electromagnetic dance, with its twenty-three billion cells discharging at specific frequencies. These discharges are measurable. Our normal waking brainwave state is primarily beta (13–40 cycles per second). Beta can be described as the state of nervous anxiety where we are ready for any low-grade activity, like driving the car, or shopping. This is the state our current Western culture runs around in. When we become more serene and relaxed in what I have been calling a state of presence, our brainwaves shift to include more alpha (8-13 cycles per second). This is the state we call peak performance. This is where artists tune in to create and athletes go to perform.

The next range on the spectrum is theta (4–7 cycles per second); this state is linked to insights, inspiration, healing, feelings of connectedness and integration. In a very informal experiment we did measuring brainwave states while companion walking with a horse, we saw a spike in theta just before the human reported feeling the connection with the horse.

The last of the measurable brainwaves is delta (½–4 cycles per second). Delta is equated with spiritual breakthroughs and the feeling of being in the driver's seat of our own consciousness.

Interestingly, when horses brainwaves have been measured, we find that they have very little beta and much higher amplitudes of alpha, theta and delta. This indicates that horses live in a very expanded state of awareness.

It is encouraging to know that the state commonly referred to as flow or coherence is a learnable state. And horses can help us get there. The noise that keeps us from tuning

The essential joy of being with horses is that it brings us in contact with the rare elements of grace, beauty, spirit and fire.

SHARON RALLS LEMON

*Being with horses,
in a state of presence,
can awaken dormant
abilities within
us . . . . Horses help
us remember how
to read the field.*

in to the bigger field occurs as busy repeated thoughts, such as our judgments, beliefs, fears, and doubts, to mention a few. These are the distractions that prevent our conscious awareness from being completely in the moment, the place where, if we listen with awareness, we can hear the voice of our own intuition and our own creative source.

Horses help us cultivate in ourselves what we need to hear in this intuitive way. They help us learn to trust the subtle images, feelings, and emotions that we begin to perceive. Through our relationship with horses, we not only have these subtle communication skills modeled for us, we have the opportunity to hone our own to use with our fellow humans.

JOHAN

Communication within the field
is instant and efficient

One evening I received a phone call from the owners of the ranch where I was boarding Johan, my Dutch Warmblood gelding. He was being leased to a young rider competing with him in order to qualify for the Jr. National Dressage Championships. The ranch owners had called to inform me of both good news and bad. The good news was that Johan had won his classes at the most recent horse show. The bad news was that when they brought him home, he was limping. They had called the veterinarian. The vet took ultrasound images of his front legs and couldn't find anything wrong. He instructed the ranch owners to give Johan anti-inflammatory drugs and keep him stalled for three weeks. When I heard this, I immediately knew the diagnosis and the treatment were wrong. I didn't know how I knew, but I was certain of it.

I decided to sit quietly and clear my mind. I needed to create a clear space—free of thoughts, fears, judgments, and beliefs—and allow the intention of connecting with my beloved Johan. I imagined a TV screen behind my eyes to see things on. In an instant, his image popped on my screen as if he was waiting for me to tune in to the right channel. Immediately I received a picture. I saw an image of him sulking in his stall and I also noticed a lump high up in his right shoulder. The lump was about the size of an orange cut in half and stuck under his skin. Then I got a clear and instant message: "There is nothing wrong with my leg."

The next day, I flew south and drove to the barn with my husband. On the way there, I told him about my message from Johan and predicted that when we got into his stall, we'd see nothing unusual in his leg and a big lump high up on his right shoulder. We arrived at his stall to find him sulking with his head in the corner, just as I had witnessed on my imaginary TV screen the night before. Johan didn't even turn to look at me when I approached. I examined him closely, felt no heat and saw no swelling in his legs. And sure enough, I found the lump high up on his right shoulder, exactly where he had shown me. I knew he needed to get out of his stall and move around to release the knotted muscle in his shoulder, so in spite of the vet's advice, I changed Johan's regime and allowed him to get out into the pasture every day. He never took another lame step.

I know receiving this form of information is usually subtle, and when it happens repeatedly I know to pay attention and respond to it. One day while in my own barn grooming a horse, I kept having an image pop into my mind of Johan

The more we accept these experiences as normal, the more they become the norm.

standing outside his closed stall door. At first, I listened to the logic of my thinking mind and dismissed the image as nonsense. My thinking mind rationalized that since I never closed the stall doors, there was no reason to consider the validity of the image. However, the picture of Johan kept popping back into my head. I finally decided to pay attention to what I was seeing in my mind. I walked around the barn to find Johan just as the picture in my head depicted: standing in front of his closed stall door, staring at it as if it would magically open. I opened the stall door, secured it, and Johan gratefully walked into his stall for his afternoon nap. How the door got closed in the first place remained a mystery.

Often during the Equine Experiential Learning workshops I conduct today, we do a debriefing activity in the classroom while the horses stay in the arena with food and water. One day, completely out of context to what we were in the process of doing, I suddenly got an image of Benson, our black pony, standing by an empty water bucket. I like to call these images I receive "news flashes." I asked my equine assistant to check the bucket and sure enough, they found Benson standing by an empty water bucket. Working with horses helps us learn to trust these experiences. And as I learned, we can overcome our doubts about these insights by approaching them with a sense of play and curiosity.

DIORA AND THE ORANGE PEELS

Diora had become a happy, mature mare, enjoying her life with our small herd of three. One afternoon I answered a knock at my front door. There stood a young woman who introduced herself as Anna. I had never met her before. She admitted she felt she was "going out on a limb and normally wouldn't knock on a stranger's door," but she wanted to share her story about my horse with me.

Anna proceeded to tell me that she'd been having dreams with a specific bay mare in them. The dreams were very pleasant and reminded her of the years when she had her own horse and would ride and hang around the barn, soaking up the "horse atmosphere." She said that one day on her way to work, while driving by our pasture, she looked up and saw "the horse in her dreams." She had no doubt that the mare in our pasture was the exact horse that was in her dreams. This was very intriguing to her, so much so that she felt motivated to come to the door of perfect strangers, despite how awkward it was to do so and how odd her story sounded. Anna proceeded to ask if it would be alright for her to come and visit the mare sometime. This did seem like a very strange introduction and request, but I had learned over the years, if something seemingly strange happened involving Diora, it's best to go with it.

Anna worked next door at a friend's inn as their head gardener, so it was easy for me to do a little investigative work to find out if she was responsible and trustworthy to be with my horse. All was favorable in that regard. It turned out that Anna also had good horse skills and didn't need my supervision, so I granted permission for her to visit the horse whenever she wanted. Diora seemed happy to have the additional attention.

Anna called me to say that every time she came to the barn to spend time with Diora, she got the feeling that Diora wanted orange peels. She said this had been going on for a while, long enough to get her attention. She wondered if orange peels were something that horses could eat, because she kept getting the feeling that Diora wanted orange peels! Amazed at the communication skills of Diora and the subtle awareness of Anna, I shared my own story of Diora's history with orange peels, how they were her favorite treat since she was a young filly, and that I knew of no other horses that desired orange peels. Anna began regularly supplying orange peels for Diora. This experience provided further validation to Anna that her willingness to follow her own curiosity and dreams can lead to a whole new world of communication, awareness, and insight.

When we tune our awareness to the subtle, the world becomes more magical and charming.

Transmitting through the field with pictures seems a logical way to communicate for prey animals. Their survival depends on their ability to communicate and mobilize quickly in order to avoid danger. This type of instant messaging is much more efficient than cumbersome, slow-moving sounds. Anna was able to "tune in" because she had an open mind and heart. Diora was simply transmitting her desires to Anna, who perceived them as images and feelings.

As in Johan's case, where he and I connected through the field, it was an intuitive feeling that led me to realize his Johan's diagnosis was inaccurate. In addition, I perceived an image, in my imagination, of Johan's cramping muscle in his shoulder, many miles away. The subsequent action ended up being the right choice for Johan while validating my perception.

SIX

The Dynamic Dance of Relationship

⁓

Through the mirror of Relationship,
I see myself. I see the other in myself and myself in others.
⁓TAT TVAM ASI⁓
Sanskrit saying, as translated by Deepak Chopra

Horses continue to help humankind evolve. Now more than ever, it seems we not only need to learn how to cooperate with one another, we need to learn to "co-operate" together. There is a big distinction between cooperation, meaning getting along, and what horses model with their *co-operation*, meaning working together as an interactive whole. We have spent decades cultivating and celebrating our individuality and the power of *me*, while neglecting the inherent power in *we*. By learning to engage in relationship with a horse in a co-operative way, we realize that attachment to our beliefs and misunderstanding the role of emotion can prevent us from gaining the broader perspective needed to work within the dynamics of a group to achieve not only our personal goals but those of the group as well. We humans can easily slip into a competitive, dominating way of interacting, trying to defend our individual beliefs. By learning the way of the horse, we can develop a greater understanding of co-operation and how to engage in a way that fosters direct communication while building connectedness and trust.

When we consciously engage with the horses from a state of presence, our awareness expands and begins to reveal a dynamic energetic dance (or conversation) between the horse and ourselves. In this way, horses provide a direct non-judgmental opportunity for us to personally see not only how these elements interact together, but how our attachments to specific beliefs and our emotions affect the energetic dance between us. The results of these conscious interactions can be very enlightening and self-empowering.

Horses use mirroring as a form of communication. When one horse perceives something of concern, the surrounding horses will respond in kind. Usually, the herd looks to the lead horse for direction and will respond to what she does. And if more than one horse is behaving in a concerned manner, and all others are looking for the reason why, the entire herd gets the benefit of many eyes and ears. They share the perceptual *power of we,* engaged and focused all together. Once they are convinced things are safe, they collectively let go of the feeling of concern, relax, and go back to a state of peace and presence.

We do not see things as they are — we see things as We are.

OLD TALMUDIC SAYING

A horse will mirror your energetic behavior. If you are tense, they will sense tension and act tense. If you are calm, they will be calmer. Horses also model for us the benefits of setting aside judgment and loosening our attachment to our beliefs—both of which act as filters that narrow our perceptions and prevent us from complete awareness. When we do this in our equine relationships, horses immediately respond differently to us, providing wonderful feedback.

Each of us is individually unique and has our own personal perspective. And at the same time, we are continuously sharing our perceptions and feelings, in that we are transmitting or broadcasting into the field around us. We have all had the experience of feeling generally uneasy around someone for no apparent reason. And we have all experienced how it feels to be around someone who is angry or unhappy and had these feelings rub off on us. Usually this happens when we are picking up (perceiving) the energy of someone else unconsciously and what we feel influences our perceptions, making us feel similarly grumpy or sad. Horses beautifully demonstrate this interconnectedness in that they respond to both seen and unseen things they perceive without the filters of judgment. This is not unlike human interactions at home and work. We, too, perceive the frustrations and fears, as well as the confidence and visions, of our co-workers and family members. The difference is, we humans often get confused and take on undue attachment to and ownership of these perceptions, especially the negative ones. When we have a strong attachment to our beliefs and perceptions, we run the risk of slipping into a "power-over" model of behaving in relationships with others. We become less cooperative and collaborative and more competitive. In addition, when we slip into this *energetic,* we resonate, or enliven these feelings in others.

Because emotions resonate in us, they occur to us as our feelings. And in a sense they are, but they may or may not have been originated by us and they are not *who* we are. They are simply what we are perceiving through our feeling body in the moment. Perceptions are not meant to linger. They are meant to inform, cause a response, and then be let go of. The process of understanding the origins of what we perceive and how we process our perceptions is where we gain self-empowerment.

In Miguel Ruiz's book *The Four Agreements,* one of the Agreements is: *Don't take things personally.* This is important because by not taking things personally, we relinquish our attachment to the limits of our personal perspective. Our awareness will be free to shift and expand. This is who we are by nature. We are part of, and continuously interacting within, the bigger whole.

While learning to listen with awareness, it helps to think of emotion as simply *energy in motion*. Emotions sometimes are generated from within, but at other times, what we perceive as a feeling is not originated solely from within us, but actually comes from another. We are effectively resonating with a feeling generated by someone else. We perceive it through the shared energetic field around us because we are all interconnected.

We are not our feelings; we have feelings. Feelings are a form of information. When we find ourselves having a strong emotion it is helpful to pause a moment and inquire as to the origin of what we are feeling. In pausing and in-quiring, we are more able to hold what we feel *lightly* and gain insight. We can then decide if a particular thought or belief is appropriate in serving our heart's intention in that moment and in relationship to our current situation. We may discover that a belief we hold was appropriate when we were 10 years old, but is not appropriate to our current worldview or our current intention.

Horses demonstrate how we send, receive, and perceive emotional information.

When we understand that we are continuously being influenced and in turn influencing the field around us, we welcome shifts in our perspective and feel empowered by our interactive influence in the field.

The Lakota Native Americans lived by a code called Circular Thinking. They understood that what they thought and did reflected back to them in relationships. "What goes around comes around." They experienced this dynamic through their relationship to nature and certainly in their re-lationships with their horses. They knew the energetic field to be influence-able and responsive.

OPALO
Circular Thinking

AT FOUR IN the morning, while making the shift from my dream state into waking, I had a profound realization. I had a clear physical feeling and understanding of how connected we all are. I clearly understood how our interconnectedness manifests in our relationships and lives. This lovely Satori that I experienced upon waking set the tone and guided my perception for the rest of the day.

My daughter was heading off to college. The process of choosing a college had a psychological and emotional impact on both her life and mine. For her, it marked the beginning of a wonderful time in young adulthood where she could be more independent, explore being out on her own, and discover more of who she was becoming. For me it marked not only a new beginning, but also the end of a significant time in my life where I had been Mommy, provider of a nurturing home, program director for family activities, and Equine Experiential Learning professional. I had been the proverbial supporter of others for 18 years. When I looked at the inevitable change approaching both our lives, I felt happy and excited. I was eager to have more time for my own interests yet also happy to see my daughter take her next big step in life.

Life isn't happening to you — it is responding to you.
RHONDA BYRNE

I looked forward to discovering what opportunities would emerge for everyone in our family. This was a positive new beginning. And at the same time, I felt great sadness about having someone I loved move away. On this particular day, the sadness had become my predominant emotion. As much as I understood that the stories and beliefs we hold and entertain in our mind create the emotions that follow, and ultimately color our perceptions, the negative thoughts kept creeping in and created a cycle of negative emotions. I struggled to keep aligned with the positive side of my story. I kept having feelings of resentment in me and around me in the field.

Entertaining these negative stories in my mind caused feelings of resentment and frustration to follow. As a result, my thoughts would creep in and make me want to avoid being with my family, who, in a circular fashion, became the triggers for these thoughts and feelings. I could see what was happening and I understood that this was a classic case of transference. This all seemed obvious once the cycle became apparent, but until it came into my full awareness, it was happening unconsciously. I was caught in a vicious cycle of negative emotions.

Later that day, I led my horse Opalo out of his pasture for our regular training session and he followed along in his usual willing fashion. As we walked down the road toward the barn, my mind wandered and I began looping again through the negative thoughts and emotions related to the changes happening in my life. Immediately, Opalo swung his head around and took an aggressive nip at my shirt-sleeve. I was surprised at this behavior; it was so out of the ordinary. Nipping wasn't something he normally did. But I didn't react to his nip nor did I take his behavior toward me personally. Instead, I stopped and paused for a minute. I knew an open heart and curious mind would allow for a clearer perspective.

I turned to Opalo and inquired out loud, "What was behind that nip?" Immediately I felt that the emotion or energy motivating his nip was resentment. I queried myself: what might he have to feel resentful about? An answer came immediately—how about being taken from his nice pasture buffet and from his friends? But then I thought, "He isn't resentful about these things on other days, why today?"

Then it dawned on me. Perhaps I had brought a cloud of unconscious "resentful" energy with me and he resonated with it. I acknowledged the resentful emotions in myself that morning. And I recognized the stories and beliefs that had prompted them. I suddenly realized that I had continued to unconsciously sound the drum of resentment at an energetic level. Meanwhile, Opalo, instead of stuffing emotions in through an intellectual filter like people tend to do, allowed his emotions to flow, to motivate his behavior. Just like the guitar string that vibrates when the corresponding piano key is sounded, Opalo seemed to be resonating with my resentment. We both had the capacity to feel resentment and I had sounded the key. I thought of all the sayings we have that describe this phenomenon: He/she is "striking a chord" in someone . . . "Like things attract". . . "We are *in sync*". . . or "We're on the same wave length." This happens for both positive and negative emotions.

After considering the possibility that Opalo's emotions were activated by me, I decided to test my theory and be responsible, or as I like to think of it, *response-able* for changing my energetics. I chose to let my resentment go, altering the emotional chord I was playing. I stayed present, did not react with retaliation to his nip, and did not entertain any feelings of regret for his behavior nor for my feelings. I was simply able to accept what was going on between us without resistance. I chose to let go of the resentment. This process allowed me to feel more peaceful. Immediately Opalo settled; he started licking and chewing—a horse's sign of acceptance. His eyes softened, and we peacefully walked to the barn where we had a wonderful time together.

Perhaps we all have an even deeper capacity to take *response-ability* in our relationships with others. If I had not been able to see or accept responsibility for my own resentment and had carried on, reacting to Opalo's actions with

You cannot always control what goes on outside. But you can always control what goes on inside.
WAYNE W. DYER

75

retaliation or reprimand, we would have stayed *in circulari-ty,* generating a negative feeling state, continuing to trigger and transfer the energy of resentment back and forth be-tween us. Instead, I was able to move to a state of presence, and curiously inquire about the energy behind the original emotion. I allowed it to inform me, which subsequently helped me make a different choice in how I wanted to be.

In Gregg Braden's book *The Divine Matrix,* he asserts that scientific evidence proves that we are all different parts of the giant fabric we call the world, universe, and life. The uni-verse is more like a hologram than we previously thought, and the "Butterfly Effect" is real and provable. The Butterfly Effect suggests that even the smallest being has an effect on everyone and everything else in the universe. In this partic-ular interaction with Opalo, I could clearly see how my ener-gy or energetic influence was manifesting in my relationship with him. Perhaps, I was being his Butterfly Effect.

This interaction became further proof to me that aware-ness is key to identifying "the energy of relationships." Learning to raise our awareness is thus rich with opportuni-ty for personal awareness and growth. The steps in this pro-cess are to first notice or acknowledge the emotion. Next, we must allow ourselves to be with what we're feeling with a curious mind and heart. We must hold these feelings lightly, with compassion and without attachment, so we may come from a place of inquiry, with an attitude of "How interesting!" rather than ownership or resistance, thinking things like "How dare he!" or "I'm really mad now!" Finally, this allows us to follow the thought thread back to the belief(s) prompting the emotion, resulting in our ability to evaluate whether those beliefs are appropriate or not for the given circumstances. Through this process, we can get closer to the emotional links that bind us together in relationships as opposed to pushing against the behavior and the underlying emotions we don't like. The way out of feelings we don't like is not to resist them, but to go through them; they are there to inform us.

Ultimately, the way to deal with resistance is to relax. . . to let go of our attachment to what we think we know. Resist the temptation to close your heart and react or retaliate; stay in an open curious state of inquiry, allowing additional perspectives to reveal themselves in your awareness. Become aware of what you may have contributed to the field and be response-able to shift your thoughts and actions, so as to influence the relationship toward the direction you'd like to see go.

Consider that what we see and experience "out there" is always being interpreted through the lens of our own limited personal experiences, emotions, and beliefs. We are all resonating with and enlivening our environment, much like

Could self-reflection be the treasure in relationships? Being responsible for (and responsive to) our inner selves is key. Being in touch with the Self that resides in our heart is one of the keys to creating change.

a radio broadcast. When we tune in to others, we experience ourselves resonating with similar feelings in them (expressed personally as emotions). Our perceptions (how we
interpret the world) are a big mirror for us to see and experience ourselves and our relationship to the whole. We are
both influenced and have influence in this dynamic dance
of relationship. Our thoughts, beliefs, and subsequent emotions color our perceptions and motivate our actions. That
day, Opalo helped me understand that "what goes around
comes around."

SEVEN
Leading While Following

Your vision will best become clear
only when you look into your heart. . .
He who looks outside, dreams.
He who looks inside, awakens.
— CARL JUNG

THE NEW FRONTIER being explored with horses takes us on an inward journey of self-awareness. This journey, if embarked upon with open mind and heart, allows subtle sense perceptions to bloom. From a state of presence, intuition and synchronicity come into our awareness with effortless grace.

When interacting with horses, we quickly learn that in order to "fix" anything "out there," we need to acknowledge that what we see in others must exist (in some form) in ourselves. Otherwise, we would not be able to recognize or perceive it in others. In order to effectively interact with or influence what we see out there, we must start by noticing our own personal relationship to it. By shifting our awareness to noticing how we respond to and interact with what appears to be happening, we gain personal responsibility. The ability to interact without taking things personally, and without judgment, enables us to refer to our heart's intention in order to guide our response(s).

Ghandi is quoted as saying, "Be the change you want to see." When interacting with horses, we have the immediate opportunity to experience our true influence within the relationship, because horses are always authentic. Horses, like people, build bonds in their relationships based on trust. A horse reads emotional and physical body language. A horse knows immediately if you are in alignment, that is, *congruent* with your heart, mind, and spirit. If these elements are not congruent (matching your inside authentic feelings, thoughts, and emotions with your outwardly expressed body language), the horse's responses to you will reflect this through restless or avoiding behaviors.

As prey animals, horses are reliant on their ability to perceive the intention of others entering their energetic field. It is because of this extraordinary ability that they can help us learn to stay in alignment with our own intention while interacting with them. They do this by responding to authentic, congruent behavior from us—and by responding differently to inauthentic or incongruent states. They read what's going on in what I call the *heart's desire* or *inner intent,*

and will detect if someone's actions are congruent with this desire or not. Being incongruent while interacting with a horse causes it to feel confused and can lead to the horse acting uneasy.

There is scientific evidence that intention has real and measurable influence in the field. In her book *The Intention Experiment*, Lynne McTaggart summarizes some of that scientific research as follows:

> *Directed intention appears to manifest itself as both electrical and magnetic energy and to produce an ordered stream of photons, visible and measurable by sensitive equipment. Perhaps our intentions also operate as highly coherent frequencies, changing the very molecular make-up and bonding of matter.*

Intention born from our heart's desire is authentic. We become aware of our authentic, heart-based intention when we are in a state of presence and awareness. And when intentions originate from this state to guide our words and actions, we are congruent. This is how trust in relationship is built and how a horse will understand and trust us the most. This is clear congruent, authentic communication.

Authenticity and congruency are important factors in building clear, trustworthy communications in all our relationships. When we interact in our relationships in an authentic and congruent way, with our actions being responsive to what is happening in the moment, we are doing what I call *leading while following*. While we are leading with our intention, we are following and responding to the moment-to-moment feedback reflected back to us in the relationship.

Authenticity builds trust in relationships.

There is an important distinction between the energy of authentic intention and that of personal will. Personal will (as opposed to willpower) is centered in our heads and is almost always accompanied by a personal attachment to an outcome. An authentic intention, on the other hand, has a feeling quality that arises from the heart. While intention may employ willpower to help focus awareness, it does not demand one outcome. Intention is more widely inclusive and so it allows our perspective to stay broader, which opens the way for effective *leading while following*.

While intention may have an intellectual component or expression, its origin is *felt* in the heart. Sheer will alone can easily start to feel like a power-over energetic that contains a strong element of individual agenda. Will is usually rooted in fear of losing something. Intention is rooted in desiring, manifesting, and/or creating something.

When interacting with horses, we can clearly see and feel a difference in their responses to intention versus personal will. For instance, if we become aware of ourselves resisting when we don't see what we intend working out, we tend to slip into willing it to happen. We then cross the line from the dynamic dance of *leading while following* over to *will* and *power-over*. From here, it may be possible to get a horse or person to do what we want, but it will not be because they have open-heartedly chosen to cooperate. The response is then a giving in because of fear or emotional discomfort.

There will likely be no foundation of trust or a deepening bond created. In fact we may get the opposite. We may get what we wanted as far as the behavior goes, but we will not have preserved a heartfelt connection that includes deeper understanding and trust. This important distinction shows us a paradox: the more we stay focused on what's not working with regard to our intention, the more we just stay attached to "what's not working." Ironically, this causes us to stay in resonance with, and subsequently help maintain, precisely what we don't want. We are prevented from *being the change we want to see.* Instead, we are staying tuned into and being *the change we don't want to see.*

There is a rhythm of exchange in all conversations. Among humans, it is a brief space in the dialogue between two people so as not to seem you are interrupting someone. With horses, there is more space in the conversation; when horses are not stressed, they carry no sense of urgency. Our aim is to build relationship based on a foundation of trust. For any horse and human to seek a connection, as opposed to imposing emotional or physical discomfort, it requires more simple curiosity on our part—more listening, more feeling, more leading while following. Ultimately, a foundation built with an intention of authentic, heartfelt, and congruent communication will yield a profound connection.

OPALO AT THE THRESHOLD OF WILL

I SAW THE DISTINCTION between intention and will and its effect on relationships clearly one day with my horse Opalo. I was in a hurry and needed to get through my barn chores quickly to get through my busy day. I did my usual whistle for the horses to come in from the pasture.

Opalo came running in first as usual. He came galloping all the way to his stall door and then abruptly stopped at the threshold staring at me. I stood at the stall door opposite him with his halter in my hand and said, "Come here." He wouldn't come over to me. I gave him my request again only firmer and with more conviction, "Come on. . . get over here." He didn't budge. Then I paused, took a breath, and reflected on what was different, what was going on, why wouldn't he come as he usually does? What was different today?

Of course, the answer came. I was very full of will and attachment to my agenda. I was in a hurry and my approach was clearly very different energetically than how I usually asked Opalo. He wasn't sure what I was doing; this wasn't an energetic manner he recognized from me and he wasn't trusting that it was safe to approach. Once I had this realization, I let go of my attachment to whether he came or not. I simply invited him to come in a much softer, more interactive way, and of course he came right over.

DIORA AND GAIL

*A change in feeling is
a change in destiny.*
NEVILLE

A T THE TIME the following story took place, I had been teaching individuals and conducting workshops in Equine Experiential Learning. By now, everyone who had already worked with Diora knew she was the consummate teacher. She was a stickler for authentic, congruent communication. I could always count on her to communicate in a clear yet gentle way. She might use a switch of her tail, a directional point with an ear, wrinkle her nose, or simply walk away if her student was not staying connected in an authentic, congruent way. The story of Gail and Diora provides a good example of how horses mirror in their behavior what it is that they are reading or otherwise perceiving in their relationships with us.

Gail came to the EquuSatori Center to participate in an *Adventures In Awareness* introductory workshop. After the initial personal introductions, a review of the AIA Safety/

Responsibility Agreement, and brief sharing of where each of us was at mentally, emotionally, and physically, we all entered the arena to meet and greet the horses.

Gail had not been completely honest with the group in her sharing of where she was emotionally. Granted, most humans don't share our emotional upsets with relative strangers, especially if we are trying to manage those upsets and move on. Gail was in that managing process.

As a workshop participant, the initial equine interaction was to consciously move toward each horse one at a time, allowing the horse to acknowledge your presence and possibly engage in an equine version of "saying hello." After acknowledging your presence, the next step was to proceed with an extended back of hand, so the horse could equally reach out to say "hello" (in horse language, this is equivalent to our handshake). With her extensive background with horses in general and Arabian horses in particular, Gail was immediately drawn to Diora, an Arabian mare. Setting her sights on Diora, she boldly walked right into Diora's space (skipping the mutual acknowledgment piece) and started scrubbing on her head with both hands. Diora, a horse who does not like her head scrubbed, quickly turned and walked away. Gail followed in a determined hot pursuit, but Diora made a get-away. Gail finally gave up and secretly felt abandoned. After witnessing the encounter, I, as the facilitator, asked Gail if she wanted to share or have help and she said no, she was fine.

After a debriefing, we moved on to another exercise—this one designed to help participants learn to develop more subtle sense perception. We call this the body scan. Gail again chose Diora as her equine partner. The horses were all at liberty, free to walk away at any time. In this state, a horse's decision to stay next to a human is largely dependent on the horse sensing a congruent heartfelt connection with their human partner. Gail was trying to follow directions but Diora kept walking away. All the other horses appeared to be falling into meditative states with the other participants, but Gail was struggling while also refusing assistance. After Diora walked away from her for the second time, Gail could no longer contain her emotions. She began to cry. We all stopped and gathered around her for support.

Gail announced that she had to "come clean" with us and share her true feelings with the group. She explained that up until that day, she was "holding up" quite well, but seeing Diora repeatedly leave her brought up some strong feelings. She was finally sharing the truth with us. She had recently been through a divorce and was feeling very abandoned by her adult children. She was feeling as if no one wanted to be with her.

Gail continued her sharing and we all listened quietly. Suddenly, Diora came, practically trotting across the arena, pushed her way into the circle, and sweetly walked directly over to Gail. She then touched Gail, placing her forehead on Gail's heart. Diora stood in that position the entire time that Gail spoke. Something had clearly shifted between Gail and Diora. Gail's "coming clean" meant she became more authentic and congruent.

The whole universe is the stage on which your mind dances with your body, guided by your heart.
YOGI WISDOM

As the day went on, Diora chose Gail for each interaction process. Gail gained a clear understanding of how her *fear of being rejected* and *feeling rejected* caused her to approach everything with a strong and controlling will. With Diora, this came off as an "I will make her obey" attitude, which Diora was not drawn to (if anything, she was repulsed by it). When Gail allowed herself to be honest, it revealed her authentic desire and intention to connect in *a heartfelt way* to others. Diora responded immediately to the energetic shift that was more congruent and authentic—a shift that Diora could perceive from across the arena!

Gail attended many more workshops over the years, and every time she came, Diora chose to work with her, often not leaving Gail's side for days. They created a remarkable bond.

As Diora perfectly demonstrated that day, horses (like humans) have trouble following incongruent messages.

Once we become more authentic in our intent and congruent in our energetic state, we become more consistent and trustworthy, which creates a deeper connection and bond with both horses and humans.

DIORA

Authentic, Congruent Communication

ONE DAY DIORA and I were working with a student in a private EFEL session, when Diora clearly demonstrated, yet again, how difficult it is for a horse to respond to incongruence.

This day, Sally stated that her intention was to focus on her free-lunging skills. Working in the confines of a 60-meter round ring, Sally wanted to ask Diora to move away from the center of the ring and toward the outer rail, moving forward in any number of gaits in response to the most subtle cues possible. Sally's hope was to accomplish this without using words or any physical tools such as a whip or vocal commands. She wanted to accomplish this by using strictly energetic intent. This was something that Diora in particular was good at and many advanced students enjoyed the opportunity to learn how to hone these skills with her.

Sally would start with the subtlest of directives to Diora, cues that would be almost imperceptible to an onlooker. This was an exercise and practice in *listening with awareness* and *leading while following,* while incorporating focused and congruent intent. In order to communicate clearly with this level of subtlety, both Diora and Sally needed a high degree of presence. I knew that if Sally made clear, authentic and congruent requests, Diora would understand and do as she was asked. This type of activity is where Diora really shines.

Sally entered the round ring and stated her intention to have Diora move out to the rail and trot around her at the furthest edge of the ring. She stepped into the middle of the ring and took a moment to center herself and connect with Diora. By moving physically to the center, Sally's expectation and stated intent was that Diora would understand her directive and comply.

When Sally made her first attempt at giving the horse a request to move, Diora seemed a bit confused. Sally then gave a more obvious directive, waving her arms a bit to signal that she wanted Diora to move away from the center over to the outer rail. Diora went out to the rail just as she was asked, took a few steps, stopped, and then calmly walked back to Sally in the center of the ring. Diora then stopped, lowered her head beside Sally and stood as if they were going to take nap together.

Both Sally and I thought this was strange behavior for Diora, who was usually quite peppy and eager to get up and go. So Sally gave it another try. Everything *looked* congruent and yet she got the same response. After repeating her efforts three or four times with the same exact results, Sally became frustrated and called for a time out. With Diora standing patiently at her side, we began an inquiry into what was happening.

Based on everything I could visually perceive, Sally seemed in alignment with her stated intention. I suspected there was more going on internally, at the energetic level, so I asked, "What are you feeling inside?" I reminded Sally that there are no wrong answers to a question like this. We were merely exploring what was going on between her and Diora, on all levels—emotional, energetic, mental, and physical. Sally got quiet, thought about it for a few moments and then confessed, "Well, if I were to tell the truth, what I really *feel* like doing with Diora today is just hanging around together. I know I came to hone my skills in round ring work, but inside I don't feel like moving her around the ring."

Aha! We had found our answer. I pointed out that wanting to hang around together was fine, but her emotions were conflicting with her other signals and sending incongruent messages to the horse. Diora was doing her best to obey both signals ("move around the round ring" but also, "stand and share space with me"). She was responding to the initial request to move off and go around the ring, but after doing that, she was trying to appease Sally's heartfelt signal to simply come over and hang out. Both Sally and I were impressed with Diora's willingness to oblige and not get too frustrated with the incongruence. Sally could see that if she aligned her emotions, intention, and her physical body language, her response from the horse would be clearer too.

There is something about the Nature of the Horse that is food for the Soul of Man . . . .

After regrouping with her new awareness about how she was incongruent, Sally became even more present and aware of her physical, emotional, and energetic states. She became more congruent. When she turned to Diora to try the round ring work again, before she even asked with a physical cue, Diora moved out to the perimeter of the ring and trotted around energetically. It took hardly any effort for Sally to keep her going and when she changed her intention to have Diora come in and hang out, Diora was right on task and responded immediately. All of Sally's requests were subsequently communicated non-verbally. It was as easy as moving a tiny feather with her breath. The communication between them appeared to be a seamless flow.

EIGHT

Congruency, Coherence, and Peak Performance

───────

A lovely horse is always an experience . . .
It is an emotional experience
of the kind that is spoiled by words.
— BERYL MARKHAM

U P UNTIL NOW, we have used the term *presence* to describe a state of being within ourselves that helps us connect to horses. There is a physiological scientific term that is a corollary to presence. That term is *coherence*.

Coherence helps us understand the physiological aspects of presence. It is helpful to understand this because the principles we are talking about when we explore communication within the energetic field are not just anecdotal or subjective. These principles are part of nature and are now understood and validated by scientific study.

The following is a scientific description of coherence from Dr. Rollin McCraty, head of research for the HeartMath Institute in Boulder Creek, California. These passages help define some of the terms I have adopted to explain what happens in horse-human relations.

The term "coherence" is used in physics to describe the ordered or constructive distribution of power within a waveform. An example of this is the Sine wave. Coherence also describes two or more waves that are either phase or frequency locked; such as when two or more of the body's oscillatory systems such as respiration and heart rhythms become entrained and oscillate at the same frequency. This is called cross-coherence.

We have also demonstrated that physiological coherence is associated with increased synchronization between the heartbeat (ECG) [electrocardiogram] and alpha rhythms in the EEG [electroencephalograph]. We found that the brain's alpha activity is naturally synchronized to the cardiac cycle. When subjects used a positive emotion refocusing technique to consciously self-generate feelings of appreciation, their heart rhythm coherence significantly increased, as did the ratio of the alpha rhythm that was synchronized to the heart.

Another related phenomenon associated with physiological coherence is resonance. In physics, resonance refers to a phenomenon whereby an unusually large vibration is produced in a system in response to a stimulus whose frequency is identical or nearly identical to the natural vibratory frequency of the system. In summary, we use the term coherence as an umbrella term to describe a physiological mode that encompasses entrainment, resonance, and synchronization, all of which emerge from the harmonious activity and interactions of the body's subsystems.

Seeing with the heart requires opening the heart . . . . It's really all about how a real sense of connectedness arises, with one another and with the world. Without that expectation of connectedness, real sensing and presencing won't occur.

FROM THE BOOK

PRESENCE

The HeartMath Institute was the perfect partner to establish that there exists energetic resonance between horses and humans. In a research project that I was a part of in 2006, my fellow EEL colleague Dr. Ellen Gerhke and I worked with the researchers at the HeartMath Institute to see if we could determine if there was any measurable energetic synchronization going on between horses and humans. This was important to us in order to validate the personal experiences that many EEL practitioners had witnessed in their own work with horses.

Our research ultimately confirmed that much of what we had experienced as feelings of connectedness, and which we had visually witnessed as connectedness between horses and humans was indeed real and measurable as coherence between horses and humans.

The first exciting thing that our research with HeartMath revealed was that when actually measured with accurate scientific equipment, coherence in horses looks almost identical to coherence in humans. A second important finding was that (unlike humans) horses stay in a coherent state most of the time. When they do move out of coherence, they are quick to return to it.

Another of our key findings was that when horses and humans were measured in the same environment at the same time while engaging in various activities together, the greatest increase in measurable, energetic synchronization between the two took place when the human was sending thoughts and feelings of appreciation to the horse. This was validating research that helped explain what had previously been consistent but anecdotal experiences for those working with horses in this way. More importantly, our research seemed to be only the tip of the iceberg.

What we saw in further studies conducted between horses and humans clearly indicated that interactions with horses can have a very positive effect on humans. Dr. Ann

Baldwin, researcher at the University of Arizona, provided additional analysis of our original HeartMath data and determined that within the original experiments, the horse(s) had moved into a state of coherence slightly (but measurably) in advance of the human(s) who also made a shift toward more coherence. This strongly implied that the coherence of the horse seemed to have influenced the human into a similar energetic state.

In Lynne McTaggart's book *The Intention Experiment*, she describes a similar pattern that scientists observed when measuring brainwaves:

> *Scientists Grinberg-Zelberbaum discovered that brainwave synchrony occurred not only between two people but between both hemispheres of the brains of the people — and the person with the most cohesive quantum wave patterns sometimes set the tempo and tended to influence the other. The most ordered brain pattern often prevailed. In many instances when one person is sending focused intention to another, their brains appear to become entrained.*

It appears that just as in the Grinberg-Zelberbaum experiments, a horse's more coherent state can influence the human's. This may help explain why it is that when we are around horses, in an open receptive state of mind (particularly in a state of presence), we feel good both physically and emotionally. It appears that just being in the resonant field of horses in a state of presence can help us shift to a state of greater coherence within ourselves.

Additional research at the HeartMath Institute has shown that the electromagnetic field of the heart organ is 5000 times stronger than that of the brain. With super sensitive SQUID (super-conducting quantum interference device) equipment, scientists are able to read this field up to ten feet away from the body. In addition, they found that the heart organ has its own nervous system and the ability to send messages to other organs in response to what it feels many seconds before the brain is involved. Evidently, our "heart field" precedes us.

As evidenced in stories such as the one with Gail and Diora, we can see that horses are reading this heart field and

The Brain gives the Heart its sight.

The Heart gives the Brain its vision
KALI

responding to it. When we are congruent with our heart, we are most authentic and trustworthy. Just as in person-to-person relationships, where it was found that *congruent hearts entrain with one* another, it seems that the same is true between horses and humans.

If we consider that throughout our entire body, we have mirror neurons designed to pick up the emotional states of others, while our heart organ is emitting an electromagnetic field many times stronger than our brain, it is not too far-fetched to believe that by honing our awareness, we can build skills to improve what we perceive in the field. We, like horses, also perceive the *field around us*. And the more we are in a heart-based state of coherence / presence, the more we can connect with others.

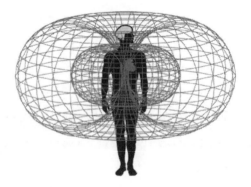

Horses help people access their natural resonant state. In the resonant state of coherence, we can access new information to regulate the body's nervous system, gain new insight and shift our perceptions.

In the illustration, we can clearly see two layers of electromagnetic field emitted from the heart. When we interact with the horses, we see the same two fields. The outer one I refer to as the acknowledgment layer, because when we approach the horse and reach this layer, they will acknowledge our presence in some way. The inner layer is much more personal. When we approach this more personal layer and stop at the edge of it, usually the horse will invite us in. Honoring this personal space shows respect and builds trust with the horse. The same is true for humans.

Control is an instrument of fear . . . . Command is an instrument of oneness.
GLENDA GREEN

COMMAND VS. CONTROL

When we are authentic, congruent, and in a state of presence, we are in our own personal peak performance state. This is a state of true personal leadership. Where we can read the field, stay in alignment with our own heart-felt intentions, and interact appropriately in the moment with others, this is true authentic leadership.

There is an important distinction to make in this context of energetic leadership. This distinction is Command versus Control. When we take command of a situation, we are accepting a role of being *responsive* to it by being *"response-able."* We are not controlling the situation; we are just *commanding* ourselves within it, in response to it . . . with intention.

In contrast, when we are trying to control something, there is usually a fear behind our action. We are being motivated by this fear. And from this place of fear, we are no longer acting from a state of presence (in the moment) but from a more narrowed personal perspective, which includes an overlay of fearful possibilities or outcomes. While fear is a very important and effective tool to move us physically out of harm's way at a moment's notice, it is not the best place to make decisions while interacting in most everyday situations.

With horses, we quickly learn that if what we are looking for is a true connection and direct energetic communication, we can never really control them (in order to achieve this or other voluntary behaviors), but we can engage them in a way that exhibits our command. This is a key element to true authentic leadership. Through interacting with and guiding the energies available in the moment, we can feel and know the difference between when we are in command mode versus control mode within ourselves.

When we command a situation, we are able to utilize intention as a guiding influence, while interacting with what is actually available to us in the moment. We have more creative options; we are listening with awareness and leading while following, without resistance to what is. In the fear-based state of control, we are clinging to the notion of what we feel should have happened or ought to be happening.

In the following story, author Glenda Green describes her personal moment of Satori, where she began to understand how to engage with *oneness* in relationship with her horse:

One day I was practicing at the arena when an old cowboy noticed some trouble I was having with my mare. Her timing was slow, and the circles she was cutting were much too large. I was struggling with all my options for control, having no success. The old man motioned for me to come over to the fence, and I was hopeful that he would have some training tips for me. He did, though it was nothing I had expected. In a Texas drawl, between puffs of a cigarette, he asked, "Honey, how much do you weigh?" I had a "Twiggy" sort of figure in those days, and I blushed to admit that I only weighed 102 pounds. Then pointing to my mare, he asked, "What makes you think you can throw around a thousand pounds of horse flesh like you're trying to do?"

I was stumped! What kind of question was that? I started to shrug it off and walk away when something inside told me that he was leading up to a point I needed to hear. This was a man who had trained champions for almost fifty years, but I couldn't tell yet whether he was about to put me down or give me the benefit of his experience. Nevertheless, I was curious enough to take my chances.

He continued. "If you make that mare choose between doing it your way or hers, she'll probably compromise and fall short somewhere in the middle. Then you'll try to make up the difference with persuasion or force. You'll never get real performance like that. The secret is to become one with the horse, so that your way is her way! Then you'll outweigh her by 102 pounds . . . and be the one in charge." I was all ears after that, and he proceeded to teach me some secrets of "oneness."

We will never control life, but we do have the power to engage in a way that allows us to be in command.

Your source of power has been established within your heart, not your mind. The mind is designed to be the servant of the heart. And the heart is much more than emotion and a circulation pump. The nervous system associated with the heart is extremely aware of subtlety and is designed to work in concert with the mind. It is from this power, at the center of our being, with the mind and heart in synchronized coherence that we tap into our peak performance state. This is where we connect with our creative source. In this place, we can command with love, perceive with a broader perspective, and feel more connected.

JOHAN AND THE CHIROPRACTOR

He who knows
others is wise.
He who knows
himself is
enlightened
LAU-TZU

ONE PARTICULAR EFEL workshop at the EquuSatori Center was attended by a wonderful group of enthusiastic women. One of these women was a chiropractor whom I shall call Nancy. She had a successful practice and had been recently expanding her work to include horses. Nancy had taken some coursework for equine chiropractic, but was finding that she experienced some horses as intimidating. In particular, the larger horses were frightening for her. Nancy's stated objective for the workshop was to confront this fear and gain some tools of understanding that would help her better connect with horses, especially those that made her fearful.

Our horse colleagues / teachers that day consisted of Benson (a black Half-Arab / half-Welsh pony gelding), Diora (our Half-Arab mare), and Johan (a large Dutch Warmblood gelding). When Nancy shared with the group that her issue was fear, I suspected at that point that she'd be attracted to Johan. Johan had previously worked through his own fear issues and I had seen many times how people somehow seemed to attract the horse that was best suited to help them, in part because of the horse's own experiences with the same or similar issues.

We began with an exercise called "Choose or Be Chosen." In this exercise, participants may choose a horse to interact with, or sometimes a horse will choose a participant. Interestingly, Nancy was clearly chosen by Johan, not only the largest horse in the herd, but also the most fearful for her, at least in the past. Johan came directly to Nancy and then stood patiently by her side. She agreed to work with him.

We had completed a didactic session with each other to shift our center of awareness from our heads to our hearts. Next, we were getting ready to begin our process of energetic body scanning with the horses, while staying in a heartfelt state of presence. Our objective was to stay grounded and use hands and focused awareness to scan both the physical bodies and energetic levels of the horses. The purpose in a body scanning interaction was to just be with the horses, not to know or do anything. We were also trying to establish a back-and-forth sensory awareness and interaction with the horses. Staying in *question* mode and being willing to suspend disbelief were key to finding this particular way of perceiving.

Once we began, I observed Nancy and could see this process was proving to be a bit of a challenge for her. I saw how difficult it was for her to quiet her continuous internal dialog (which we all have). She kept talking about what she was *physically* feeling in Johan's spine. Her awareness was emanating from the chiropractic interpretations she was referencing from her past experience. She was stuck in her head, perceiving Johan only through the lens of her chiropractic training. She was identifying what was out of alignment and describing which tools she would typically use to adjust the spine back into place.

At one point Nancy found a spot on Johan's neck that she felt could be adjusted if she could just manipulate it a bit. As she moved her hands over this spot with the intention of "fixing it," Johan pulled back and started to walk away. Nancy didn't pursue him; she just stayed where she was, looking puzzled. Johan paused and then, on his own, returned to her and she began the exercise again, proceeding just as before. Again, when she got to the spot on his neck, he pulled back and walked away. We noticed that as soon as she would quit *doing*—trying to *fix* and *control* the process—Johan would return and stand next to her again. This exchange continued three or four times until finally Nancy was frustrated and asked for help.

Nancy shared that she didn't understand why Johan was leaving, or coming back for that matter. I suggested that she not talk or share while she worked with him, just center and ground herself, then scan his body from a loving place of compassion and wonderment. I asked her to listen with *awareness,* and let each of her movements be guided by *impulses from within her heart* and to stay in a process of *inquiry,* not one of trying to *know.* She was to allow her responses to be guided by the reactions of the horse, not those of her mind. Her new approach was to move at the pace of *inner* guidance and not with a sense of already knowing.

As she returned to Johan with this approach as her guide, we all witnessed a big shift. It appeared that the quality of both her intention and awareness had changed. And she proceeded to engage in a beautiful energetic dance with Johan. Nancy then began a subtle interaction of heartfelt touch with Johan's whole body. She was connected to his every breath. She stayed in inquiry with his every move. Johan proceeded to drop his head and let his ears lop to the sides; his eyes went to half-mast and his breathing slowed. He clearly went to what we call "the zone," trusting Nancy's every move. It was a beautiful sight to see—the two of them *being* together in this way. Then, as Nancy's hands moved over the troubled spot on his neck, I saw her simply hold the area between her hands as if she had a baby bird in them, supporting it with reverence, inquiry, and awe. After a minute of this, Johan gently brought his neck around to the side where Nancy was, as if to say "thank you," and as he did this, his vertebrae visibly and audibly moved back into its correct place. Right there between Nancy's hands, his neck corrected itself!

I was able to achieve more and more insight into each of them . . . so much so that when it was time to leave the pasture of each, I did so not only with their physical images on film and in my head, but with deep feelings for each horse in my heart.

ROBERT VAVRA, *Premier Photographer of Horses*

Nancy melted into tears, she was so moved by what she had just experienced with Johan. Johan had beautifully demonstrated the healing power of true connectedness. *When our impulse to control is what we are leading with, the deeper connection, where trust is gained, is lost.* Nancy had experienced a much deeper layer of connectedness and a new way of being, grounded in the process of relating from her heart.

Johan could not trust Nancy enough to fully relax until she was totally and authentically present, listening without an agenda, and showing up with real compassion. Johan had acknowledged Nancy's healing presence and she beautifully demonstrated another way of being in relationship that is more interactive and cooperative. To me, this interaction was an example of the power of presence and listening with awareness to the dynamic dance of energy in relationship. And in this place, neither Nancy nor Johan felt any fear.

When someone asks us for help, many times we move directly into our heads to figure out their problem and decide what we think needs to be fixed and how. What the above story illustrates is that all bodies have an inner directive for healing and balance. By being grounded and centered while allowing our awareness to expand, we can engage with more compassion and we can more effectively and directly help others. By expanding our perception,

Horses beautifully demonstrate that security and trust are developed in relationships where authentic heart-based intention is the guiding force.

listening with awareness, and loosening our attachment to what we think we know, our intuition and inner guidance are more available to influence our actions. When this happens, things unfold with less stress, and with a sense of being in flow. We begin interacting with our world in a more co-creative way.

An offering of help to another, without attachment to outcome or a need to control the process, allows the other to accept the help knowing it comes from a trustworthy place. As Johan demonstrated, by coming back to be with Nancy of his own free will, help becomes a co-operative process rather than a one-way download of advice laced with personal attachment. At some level, our body wisdom knows that actions coming from a place of personal attachment and agenda are limited by a narrowed field of awareness. Horses don't play by these rules. The only way to get a horse to say yes and engage with you of its own free will is without personal attachment.

Listening with awareness allows our actions to rise from an inquisitive, heartfelt space.

NINE
Authentic Leadership

*Not just any feeling will do.
The ones that create must be without
ego or judgment. We must become
in our lives the things that we
choose to experience as our world.*

─GREGG BRADEN─
The Divine Matrix

We can appear free in the sense of no one is controlling us, yet our actions are completely predetermined by our habitual ways of thinking and acting in reaction to our circumstances.

PRESENCE

Leadership has been described as the ability of one individual to enroll others in a certain vision or task. What horses will teach are the qualities one must embody in order to enroll others and play the role of leader. While each herd of horses has clear, consistent leaders, each individual adult member of that herd has the capacity to act as leader if and when necessary. This is the beauty of a "shared" leadership model, based on leadership as a set of leadership *qualities*, distinct from mere *actions*. The qualities that comprise true, authentic leadership are ones that we are all capable of. Conscious interactions with horses hone our awareness of the personal qualities and interpersonal skills necessary to build the trust and connection in relationships that enable us to step into an empowered place of leadership.

Horses live in the moment. Because they are prey animals, they must continuously be aware of any changes in the interrelational dynamics (which is the glue) within their herd. The role that each horse plays in relationship to others in the herd is generated in every moment; thus, playing the role of leader in a relationship with a horse is part of a continuous energetic conversation. It's not like having a boss at work, where the boss is still the boss the next day when you return to work. When dealing with a horse, the leadership role must be continually re-established, through the expression of the core leadership qualities and behaviors. Just because you held the position yesterday or earlier in the same day, the horse does not assume you are still holding that position in the current moment. Each role played in the herd is never taken for granted. It is always generated in the moment, in relation to each other and in relation to what is going on in the environment.

The safest, most harmonious and influential role a human can play while engaging with a horse is that of leader.

Presence, Awareness, Intention, and Congruent Communication comprise the core qualities that must be embodied first to enable a horse to identify and respond to us as leader. These qualities are part of the energetic profile that a horse identifies as leadership and agrees to willingly follow.

These elements not only build more trust in relationships, they enable us to see what is needed in the moment, in the here and now, instead of acting out our own personal histories. This type of authentic leadership engages the wisdom and talents of the group more than relying only on one individual leader's perspective all the time.

Much has been written about the subject of leadership and horses; so much so that many EFEL programs have leadership skill-building at their core. It is not necessary to be a rider to hone these qualities essential to leadership. While interaction with horses by no means requires riding them, when we do decide to ride, we up the game. Understanding the influence our mind, emotions, and physical actions have on the horse's behavior, as we place ourselves on their back with the intention of asking them to follow our directives, becomes very important for our own safety and that of the horse.

In the following passage from his book *The Ethics and Passions of Dressage,* equestrian master teacher Charles De Kunffy eloquently describes the influence a conscious relationship with horses can have on one's character:

For centuries, horses were a means to educate the elite in all societies where the horse was known. They were man's partners, enhancing his status not only by their imposing sight, but by conveying to the beholder that in the saddle an equestrian, in all his virtue, was enthroned. . . . For it was only through the training of a horse, through riding one, that the virtues of a man could emerge. In ages past, it was believed that character develops by first-hand experience and cannot be formed by secondary, theoretical learning . . . In short, one could not talk a good equestrian line.

The horse could and did give a man a total education. He had to be tamed and befriended, and could not be fooled by honeyed words.

What De Kunffy describes is not the type of relationship that comes with being a bigger, more physically powerful entity that powers over another or scares someone into action. Rather, it speaks to a set of leadership qualities that evoke trust and connection with another being.

By learning to be responsible for our own perceptions and energetic states—physically, emotionally, and spiritually—we are able to build our skills of self-awareness and other-awareness, which enables us to respond more appropriately to what is happening in any moment. Perhaps most importantly, it supports our ability to exhibit these qualities in the face of fear. While fear is a natural emotional state designed to make us take immediate action and protect us from undue harm, it often overrides our other skills. Actions taken from a state of fear can lead to risk of bad, even dangerous, decision-making. By cultivating the *qualities* of authentic leadership, one does not necessarily avoid or eliminate fear, but one can show up in the present moment, in the face of fear, and exhibit awareness, congruence, presence, and clarity of intention. This is authentic leadership at its core. No one helped me learn this more quickly or intensely than my horse Johan, under saddle.

JOHAN HELPS ME UNDERSTAND AUTHENTIC LEADERSHIP

I had been looking for a long time for the perfect equine partner to further develop my classical riding skills. I was thrilled when I was finally led to Johan. Through a wonderful unfolding of synchronistic events, I acquired Johan as my perfect dressage partner. After bringing him home, we enjoyed a month or so of getting to know each other in the safety of the arena. The next step was to go out on the trails—to balance arena work with hill climbing and open hacking.

As we are liberated from our own fear, our presence liberates others automatically.
NELSON MANDELA

During our getting-acquainted phase, it became clear to me that Johan looked brave on the outside, but when taken out of his comfort zone of arena and barn setting, he was really not so brave after all. I spoke further with Johan's previous owner, and she told me that Johan had bucked her off two times while on trail rides. At first, when hearing this, I figured he was probably just a young colt kicking up his heels, but now, after getting to know him more, I realized that Johan's fear issues were probably the main reason for the buck-offs.

Johan was, and still is, a very athletic horse. In his prime, he could roll on the ground, flip over from side to side, and directly leap up onto his feet, rear up as high as he could, land and then buck over his head with a big twist. Then he would take off running, all before you could count to four!

When I brought Johan home, he was a six-year-old, 1,250–pound "moving machine." He was a well-balanced and exuberant horse. When he took off running beside me, the ground would actually rumble. When riding him in an arena, he never said no to anything I'd ask. Johan had a presence. He only balked at one thing—the invitation to leave the familiar comfort of the barn and arena. When Johan became afraid, a palpable jolt of fear, equal to his size and power, would be sent through the air, and anyone in that shared space could feel it. I quickly realized that in order to help guide him past his fear, I would have to first learn to deal with my own. Only when I could maintain an even greater amount of calm and clear intention in the presence of his fear, could I even begin to draw him toward a more calm state.

One day I was feeling particularly calm, strong, and clear. After our arena workout, I rode him up the road, away from the barn. When we got to the edge of his comfort bubble, I backed him up just a bit and asked him to calmly stand. He immediately began to act out his fear in an effort to convince me that we should go home. I maintained my calm and kept my focused intention on inviting him to be calm with me and to just stand in one place. My intention needed to be a bigger field than Johan's fear.

At first, this approach to working with Johan's fear, a process of dissecting and desensitizing the problem, didn't really work as well as I'd hoped. Uneasy thoughts crept into my mind and I felt a little afraid myself. I also began to feel frustrated and wanted this phase of his training to be over already. In order to prevent fear from getting a foothold, I would need to focus even more of my awareness on the present moment, and then generate the energetic feeling I wanted. Standing there with Johan, at the edge of his comfort zone, I remained calm, open, and continually questioning . . . *What is the appropriate action right now?*

Suddenly, a big shift took place and Johan began to listen and respond. The shift happened precisely when I gave up my *attachment* to the outcome. When I dropped the "you WILL do this" in my own mind, Johan began to relax, more and more by the minute. Without that pressure, we both became more present and engaged in an in-depth energetic conversation. I continued with my intention of sensing exactly where, in relation to the barn, he could maintain his sense of calm. I invited him to take one more step away from the barn and to be calm there as well. He continued to respond, as I stayed present with him. Together, one step at a time, we traveled up the road further and further from the barn. In a few minutes, we were out having a trail ride that we both enjoyed.

After that day, neither of us balked about leaving the barn and I learned a big lesson in how to deal with my fear. Fear invites us to be more present. No one wants to stay in the narrowed state of awareness that allows fear to take hold, especially a horse. When I was able to step into a leadership role and demonstrate energetically, physically, and with clear congruent intention that there was nothing to be afraid of, Johan decided that it felt better to stay calm with me rather than continue to be in fear.

Becoming an *energetic leader* in my work with Johan would prove to be an important capability throughout my horse career. I learned that the embodiment of these authentic leadership qualities was the most powerful form of leadership I, or anyone, could develop, because these qualities inspire the very trust that is essential in any situation that demands leadership, whether among horses or humans.

Leadership should also be thought of as dynamic. Ideally, we can all play a leadership role when necessary. In some situations giving strong directives to avoid physical danger might be called for, while in other instances, deeply listening and responding to the situation at hand might be more appropriate. In the prior instance, Johan needed me to lead with clear directives and inner calm and confidence to help him through his fearful apprehension. The next example of leadership demonstrates how employing *listening with awareness* can lead to implementing inventive co-creative solutions in an emergency situation.

BENSON AND THE HEALING POWER OF MUSIC

Benson was a very self-sufficient pony. In our Equine Facilitated Experiential Learning workshops, he was frequently the one to connect with anyone having an emotional upset, often before the human group was aware of it. He was very calm and grounded. He was one of those horses that we refer to as a "confidence builder" for people. It was not uncommon for him to transmit pictures as a way of communicating. His messages were always of a practical nature, like pointing out an empty water bucket. He never tried to get special attention, he was a caregiver.

When I first acquired Benson and brought him home, I was concerned about how and when to integrate him into the herd with the big horses. He was just five years-old and only 13 hands tall (a hand is 4″) while the other horses were considerably larger. I was slowly integrating him with the others one at a time, letting them get acquainted individually before putting them all together. At night I would put each horse in a stall with large walkout runs. This way I could control the amount and content of what they ate. By day, they were in large pastures. I left the barn one evening, considering putting them all together the next day, but wasn't feeling sure yet.

The next morning, I came down to the barn to find that during the night, Benson had cleverly taken all the paddock gates off their hinges, allowing all the horses to be together. I found them all peacefully huddled up together in one stall. He clearly showed me that the time was right and they were ready to be together. He never dismantled the gates again . . . clever fellow.

Years later, while preparing for a lesson with a riding student, I could see something was very wrong with Benson. He was thrashing around on the floor of his stall, getting up, fiercely pawing the ground with his front legs and then dropping to roll again. Benson was clearly in severe pain from colic. I immediately called the veterinarian and proceeded to halter him to get him walking instead of thrashing.

My young student Sera was scheduled to have a lesson with Benson at the same time I had discovered him struggling. Sera and her mother were probably just about to arrive. Sera was 10 years old and had been working with me for a couple of years. She had developed a nice, sensitive approach to her horsemanship. Often while Sera and I were having a lesson, her mother, Shaun, was off hanging out with the other horses. Eventually Shaun developed an uncanny connection to the horses. Many times while I was working with Sera, Shaun would pick up on all types of subtle things going on with the others. I always welcomed Shaun's input on things at the barn.

In addition to her astute intuition, Shaun brought a wealth of alternative healthcare knowledge, so I was a bit relieved when they drove up. As soon as they arrived, I explained what was going on with Benson and offered that they could stay and help me create an atmosphere of love and support for him until the vet arrived. Without hesitation they were onboard to help.

At first I was overcome with fear and concern for Benson's life; however, I knew that staying dialed in to the fear would not be helpful. I regained my sense of calm by taking some deep breaths and directing my intention to tuning in and listening with awareness. The immediate question was, "What can I do to help him until the vet arrives?"

From a calmer state, an answer came. I had a number of essential oils on hand that I knew were effective for calming nerves and giving support to the digestive tract. Shaun worked as my "go-for person" and brought the oils out to

The greatness of a nation and its moral progress can be judged by the way it's animals are treated.
MAHATMA GANDI

131

Benson and me. At this point, Sera seemed like she was not worried. She disappeared, wandering around the barn area, playing with the cats, and exploring.

Prior to the oils arriving, Benson had been wanting to drop to the ground immediately if I stopped walking him. When the oils arrived, he directed his attention toward them. I held out the bottles of oil one at a time for him to smell. He was willing to stop and smell the oils without going down. I wanted to see which one he was most attracted to. After investigating two or three, he was clearly most interested in the peppermint oil. He returned to it many times, putting his ears up while smelling it. I liked his choice—peppermint is good for settling digestion. I figured that if nothing else, the tingling sensation of the peppermint would put his attention on the area that needed relief.

After I applied some oil to his belly, Benson resumed trying to get down to thrash on the ground. It took every ounce of my attention and effort to keep him up and walking. My thoughts started drifting to stories I'd heard of other colic situations, how long and stressful they had been, some lasting for days. And why hasn't the vet called me back yet! This was not an emotional place from which I could be an effective leader. I could not lead while following my emotions. Once again, I had to catch my runaway thoughts and redirect them back to a more positive place.

At this point, I felt as if all I could do was surrender; not to his pain and suffering, but to faith in knowing that we could find a path to healing for Benson. I put my arm over his neck and began to stroke him with the same loving assurance I would give my own child. I felt very nurturing and began to imagine that I was in some way "melding" with him. I sensed that he was worried and feeling panic. I thought, "If words have resonant power inherent in them, I should not hold back my urge to speak to him." I verbalized out loud that I was there for him and together we would get through this. I allowed compassion to fill my heart rather than fear, and consciously spoke to him only when I was feeling confident.

Once I moved from fear to compassion, things started to shift for me. I felt stronger emotionally. When I spoke to Benson, I wasn't pretending when I said, "Things will be all right," as I knew they would truly be. At this point, the thought occurred to me that all of us, in our true nature, are hardwired for balance and harmony. Balance and harmony are part of nature and lie at the core of everyone's existence. This has to be true—or else we wouldn't know when we weren't in balance and harmony. Similarly, health is inherent in everyone because we all have an innate sense of how to heal. Everybody is wired to heal and Benson was no exception. I was offering myself to serve in his healing process, whatever that might be. From this open-minded and open-hearted place, I immediately saw him settle a bit and we continued to walk.

Then another thought popped into my head, one that was so out of context from my current train of thinking that I paid special attention to it. My thought was, "Benson would like me to play the music *Sacred Chants of Mother Divine* in the barn." These are beautiful ancient Vedic chants, sung in Sanskrit. They have been utilized for thousands of years as a tool for calling body and soul back into coherent resonance with divine nature. I often played this music in the barn while I worked or during workshops. Of all the horses, Benson in particular seemed to always respond to the music by becoming calm and peaceful while it was playing.

Shaun put the music on—and immediately Benson made an abrupt U-turn. He briskly walked over to the end of the arena and positioned himself directly under the speaker. Prior to hearing the music, he had been very agitated, but with the music raining down on him, he stood still, lopped his ears, dropped his head, closed his eyes, and listened.

After a few minutes, Shaun and I began a process called "belly lifting." The process is done with two people, one on each side of the horse. With hands clasped under his belly, we gave gentle lifts upward, then lowered and slid our hands back toward his tail a bit and lifted again. Sometimes this process helps release the pressure and tension of a sore, bloated belly. Benson seemed to welcome our healing touch, and all the while, he never moved a foot or twitched an ear. Together, while Shaun and I lifted, we all listened to the beautiful music.

After thirty minutes, Sera reappeared. She calmly came up to us and said, "I think Benson wants to play with Opie" (Opalo was a yearling at the time). I inquired as to how she knew this and she said, "I don't know, I just think that's what he wants now." In the spirit of shared leadership and honoring information from any source, I suggested she go ahead and open the arena gate to the barn aisle. I took off Benson's halter as a signal that he could move around as he pleased. As soon as I took it off, Benson briskly walked out of the arena and over to where Opie was standing. They sniffed noses, Benson with ears perky as if inviting his young mate to play. At this point we walked the two of them back to the arena where they played and raced around joyfully. It appeared that Benson had completely recovered from his bout with colic.

I assumed that the vet would be arriving soon and would further confirm what seemed to be obvious at this point, but he never showed up. I specifically called this vet because of his quick response time, but not only didn't he show, he didn't even call. The next couple of days I kept a watchful eye on Benson. He stayed happy as could be from then on.

When we are consumed by fear or strongly attached to a specific belief, we narrow our perceptions and our possibilities.

We also narrow our access to the co-creative source.

Ideally, emotions are a source of information just like hearing or sight.

Emotions should not be the sole driver of our actions.

A few weeks later, the vet came out for a routine visit and I mentioned that I had phoned him, with no response. He said he never received the call. This is the only time in 40 years that my call to a vet hadn't gotten through. There was no chance that it was a misdial because I had his number on my phone's speed dial and I left a message. I believe the vet was being honest with me. I was left to wonder if perhaps it all turned out just the way it was supposed to, and that at some level we all, including Benson, knew the vet would not be necessary.

That day, Shaun, Sera, and I listened to our intuition. Although I was taking the lead in the situation, we all shared in the leadership process at different times. We listened to the subtle impulses and ideas that whispered to us when we were calm. We got very clear confirmation from Benson's responses. It was a perfect example of *listening with awareness* to our inner and outer stimuli. Leading the group that day was most definitely a co-creative process. While we can't say our success was due to any single thing we did, the combination of music, essential oils, and our healing touch seemed to be exactly what was called for. What we do know is that events like these are inspiring, filling us with positive energy and a sense that miracles are possible.

TEN

Co-Creativity:
The Ultimate End Game. . .

~

*Disregard appearances, conditions, in fact
disregard all evidence of your senses that deny the
fulfillment of your desire . . . rest in the
assumption that you already are what you want to be.
For in that determined assumption,
you and your infinite being are merged in creative
unity . . . with your infinite being, all things are possible.*

~NEVILLE~

*Wherever man has
left his footprint
in the long ascent
from barbarism to
civilization we will
find the hoofprint of
the horse beside it.*
JOHN TROTWOOD
MOORE

THE WAY OF THE HORSE is an ongoing, dynamic, co-creative, and interactive relationship that includes authentic, congruent communication. When we approach all aspects of life from a state of presence, a beautiful expanded awareness emerges in us and we begin to see the co-creative effect that intention has on our reality. When we engage with horses from this state of being, they interact with us in an effortless, dynamic dance—responding to us with more and more levels of subtlety.

Science has proven that the mere act of observing something has a measurable effect on that *something*. Much has been written about this. Again science is proving what ancient religion has been proclaiming. The Vedic sutra, *San Kalpa*, is a Sanskrit word which roughly means *our intentions have infinite organizing power, and intent weaves the fabric of the universe.*

Indeed, there have been many studies done providing evidence that we are all connected and engaged with each other in relationship, connected by a unifying field. Our consciousness and intentions have an influence in this field. One of the more notable research experiments in this area was done by Karl Pribram and other researchers in 1972, involving 24 cities in the U.S. They successfully employed Transcendental Meditation (TM) to measurably reduce violence. Scientific research has since discovered that the minimum number of people required to "jump-start" a change in consciousness is the square root of 1% of the population involved.

Think of the implications of this with regard to our families, businesses, and even our politics. Taking responsibility for ourselves—being response-able to and for our perceptions and intentions—is very empowering. At some level, we all know these things to be true and most of us at one time or another have felt ourselves in the flow and tapped in to our own creativity. What the new emerging Equine Facilitated Experiential Learning work offers us is an opportunity to practice and hone the skills related to this process of self-empowerment.

When I am able to slip into the easy state-of-being commonly referred to as *flow*, while working around the barn, I notice all kinds of synchronistic events. Often when I'm finishing up my chores and shifting my intention to choosing a horse to ride, I'll walk down the barn aisle to find that particular horse waiting in his stall or walking back to the barn, just as I approach with the intention of calling him in.

In the ancient Vedic text, there is another Sutra that describes this concept—*Ritam*. It seems the ancients knew that when we understand ourselves to be connected to the unifying field that contains us all, perception shifts. We can often, as author Deepak Chopra puts it, "access the conspiracy of improbabilities," implying that in order to allow for something new to enter our awareness, certain elements within ourselves must be present. Chopra claims that one of the keys to accessing this awareness is to "change our interpretation of past events in order to create change." Again, this is a confirmation that by loosening our attachment to judgment and beliefs, we can bring more of our conscious awareness to the present moment and dwell in that state of being we call presence.

When we are fully present, it becomes clear that our attachment to beliefs and judgments, and our busy runaway minds are the main reasons we lose our sense of connectedness to our creative source. Judgment, a form of "already knowing," narrows our field of perception and receptivity. This is probably the opposite of creativity. Creativity comes from residing in a state of "*not* knowing"; it requires a lack of attachment to an outcome, and an element of curiosity and play combined. Lynn Bylined, citing author Marilyn Ferguson, writes:

> *Marilyn eloquently describes a key element of the creative process of visionaries — 'If you make peace with the unknown, it becomes your guide. The guessing, refined by the feedback of experiment, becomes intuition; explored and acted upon, becomes high instinct."*

Horses help us cultivate more sensitivity by interacting and responding to us in new, more nuanced ways when we engage them with an open mind and open-hearted presence.

When we tune in to this place within ourselves, we connect to our creative source. It facilitates our ability to engage in a co-creative way in relationship (to anyone or anything) and in the moment. Whether the purpose is to find a creative solution while training a horse, to find a new perspective in a business situation, to solve a family dilemma, or simply to create beautiful artwork or music, this ability is a central component. The ability to think out-of-the-box and disengage from our usual perspective requires us to tune in, with curiosity, to a state of presence, which includes trust, lack of judgment, and non-attachment to outcome.

We have all done this before—but horses are invaluable and fun to practice these skills with. When we engage with horses in this way, magic does happen.

DIORA REVEALS THE MAGNET
Presence, Awe and Wonder

One day while I was out in the barn doing chores and hanging around with the horses, I had a very sweet and profound experience with Diora that demonstrated what is possible when we connect from a state of presence.

I was out in the pasture with the horses and I noticed that Johan had lost the therapeutic magnet he normally wore around his hoof. This rather expensive magnet was specifically designed to help horses alleviate arthritis. Johan had been wearing it all the time, and so it was getting quite worn and tattered. I hoped to find it, somewhere, camouflaged in the blanket of green grass among the six acres of pasture the horses roamed around in.

I wasn't particularly upset, as I knew it was not quite like finding the proverbial needle in a haystack, but almost. I figured I was going to spend a lot of time combing the acres of tall grass. I started slowly walking in a methodical pattern, back and forth, scanning the ground. Not long into my walk, I became distracted by what a beautiful day it was. The horses looked so striking as they peacefully walked around in the pasture. I relaxed, allowing myself to be filled with gratitude as I wandered, fully present, in this

Creativity is not inspired by the pressure of time but by the freedom of playfulness and fun. The act of focusing our consciousness is an act of creation. Consciousness creates!

GREGG BRADEN
The Divine Matrix

145

lovely field, soaking up the vibe of the horses and nature. On this day, it felt easy to stay in a state of presence while I continued my search.

I soon came upon Diora, who was calmly munching grass. When I looked at her, the thought occurred to me, "I'll bet she knows every square inch of this pasture. She has been walking back and forth munching grass across every bit of it for years. I'll bet she knows exactly where the magnet is." I said to her, "Diora, how about taking me to the magnet?" At the same time I said this to her, I had a clear picture in my mind of what the magnet looked like and I fully believed it was possible for her to direct me to it.

Diora casually picked up her head, took a couple of steps toward me (enough to engage me in a *companion walk* with her) and then she started moving out into the pasture. I followed her lead with curiosity. Sure enough, she walked me right over to the magnet about 25 yards from where she was initially grazing. She put her head down and started munching grass right next to where it lay. I was so impressed and grateful! I gave her a big hug and told her how much I appreciated her.

We are normally so preoccupied with busy thoughts and repeating patterns in our minds that we forget to take the time to relax and make mental room for new ideas to reveal themselves to us.

But when we do, when we are tuned in to the Zero Point Field, according to systems theorist Ervin Laszlo, "It is as though we are a radio and our 'bandwidth' expands. The receptive patches in our brains become more receptive to a higher number of wavelengths when we tune into the Zero Point Field." If Dr. Laszlo's metaphor is correct and we are like radio tuners who stay tuned in to only a limited range of frequencies, any time we direct our awareness to an alternative state of consciousness, we can, in essence, change the radio dial to a wider frequency. That day in the pasture with Diora, when I relaxed and loosened my grip on how I thought I would find the magnet, another idea was able to come to me: "Why not employ the wisdom of the horse?" I had tapped into my own creative *source* with a spirit of fun and curiosity and I ended up finding a new, creative solution.

Presence and Awareness create an opening for Creativity.

Scientific studies have shown that our ability to pick up signals (expanding our bandwidth) increases during deep, interpersonal connection. When two people 'relax' their bandwidths together (i.e., their judgments and noisy thoughts) and set out to establish some kind of deep connection with intention and listening with awareness, their brain patterns become highly synchronized.

Author and lecturer Wayne Dyer has been inspiring people to get in the driver's seat of their own lives for decades.

He created wonderful spiritual roadmaps to inspire creativity and self-empowerment. He eloquently pointed out that, "Everything we see, was once imagined" and "You'll see it when you believe it."

Nowhere have these concepts been more immediately evident to me than when interacting with horses. I have yet to find a level of subtlety at which horses don't meet us when we engage with them from a gentle, peaceful state of presence. From here, we find connection to our own creativity. When we look at each present moment anew with an open mind and heart, the true nature of what is possible in the moment reveals itself to us. When we bring our *intention* to the mix, nature responds . . . and often we will be inspired with awe and wonder at what transpires.

The following is an example of one way in which an intention of mine interacted with the field and expressed itself as a wonderful synchronicity between my dog and me. It happened when I was backing up my truck toward my trailer to hitch the two together. I paused for a minute and wondered to myself why it was that sometimes I could back directly up to the trailer, perfectly aligning the ball on the truck under the hitch of the trailer in one straight shot, while at other times, I had to do multiple back and forth adjustments, getting in and out of the truck to assess how much correction to make, while becoming frustrated in the

Not just any feeling will do. The ones that create must be without ego or judgment.
We must become in our lives the things that we choose to experience as our world.
GREGG BRADEN

process. As soon as I asked myself the question, an inner dialogue began to provide my answer. I recalled the times when it just worked, and I know that when this happened, I was usually in an open-minded state of presence. I *believed* it was possible and I *expected* to get the job done directly and easily.

The thought process I had around hitching up the trailer prompted me to see that if it's true that we are all interconnected, then intelligence, in the form of information, could influence my awareness in any number of ways. In the realm of interconnectedness, *anything* could be employed to communicate in the field, through the phenomenon we call synchronicity.

I decided to put my theory to the test. I felt I was in a sufficiently open state of presence and I believed it was possible I could tap into the synchronicity of the field. I was unattached to the ultimate outcome and was experimenting with a spirit of curiosity and playfulness. I put the truck into reverse and began backing up toward my trailer. I slowed down as I got into range of the trailer's hitch receptacle, and when it seemed like I was close to lining up the ball and hitch, I became aware of a bird chirping in the hedge. This slight distraction slowed me down a bit more.

Then all of a sudden, Sammy, my Samoyed dog who had been standing off to the side of the truck, let out a single bark. I felt tickled by this and said to myself, "I'll take that as my cue." I stopped, got out of the truck and walked over to the front of the trailer. Sure enough, there was the trailer's ball, perfectly aligned right under the hitch! What fun this was. I could hardly believe it. It felt so easy, effortless, and magical. Then doubting thoughts crept in, suggesting that it was just a fluke. But there was no denying what had just happened.

What I see in nature is not the idea of controlling by cutting out and killing life — but living within a form of balance and co-operation.

A few weeks later, I was once again going through the same process of hitching up the truck and trailer. I consciously repeated the process, again generating the same feeling state I had the first time. Equally unattached to the outcome, I was simply having fun. Again, Sammy let out a bark as I backed up the truck, only this time he was nowhere nearby. Still, I took his bark as a sign, stopped backing up, and got out to see how close I might be to lining up the truck and trailer hitch. Sure enough, there it was again, in perfect alignment. This time I chuckled out loud and stopped doubting. This same alignment happened one more time a few weeks later, and it officially became my new *expected* standard. Now, I hitch up directly about 90% of the time, relying on my own belief in my ability to guide my otherwise blind lining-up of truck and trailer. I learned that the combination of my state of mind and my expectation was influencing my ability to respond and easily perform in a way that was congruent with my intention. I also saw that the birds, the dog, and who knows what else could all be responding as part of a unified dynamic interaction.

THE RUNAWAY MARES
Synchronicity, Awe and Wonder

Recently my husband Richard and I had listened to Deepak Chopra's book on tape, *The Spontaneous Fulfillment of Desire*. In this, Chopra eloquently describes how to access the creative forces of nature in order to co-create the lives we truly desire. He explains the origin and meaning of the Hindu Sutras, which are concepts from the ancient Vedas. It has long been believed that when these Sanskrit Sutra words or phrases are spoken, they create the physical sounds, which in turn resonate in the body and out into the energy field that surrounds us all. The sounds created by these words invoke the correlating principles they represent and bring them into our awareness. If these Sutras are spoken with intention, they evoke, or resonate, specific qualities of consciousness in those who practice saying them. I witnessed the essence of two of these Sutras in events that took place one summer afternoon, which I will describe in a moment.

The first sutra, *Aham Brahmasmi*, means "the core of my being is the ultimate reality, the root and ground of the

*We must let go
of our attachment
to what we think
we know in order
to discover
something new.*

universe, the source of all that exists. It is at one with the core of the entire Universe. This conscious intelligence field is the wellspring of the cosmos." Many people have come to consider this to be true based on their personal experience as well as discoveries made by modern science about the Zero Point Field. Indeed, we are all part of this field, interacting with it all the time, whether we are thinking about it or not. It connects us all. It is the ultimate field of all possibility.

Another sutra is *Ritam*, which means, "I am awake to coincidences and know that they are messages from our higher consciousness. I access the conspiracy of improbabilities and I flow with the cosmic dance." In other words, to change your life, change your patterns. We can see new patterns in coincidences. When moving in rhythm with the universe, one may notice things that others don't.

Both these sutras seemed to hold sway on two events that occurred one day in my life. The first began when my husband and I had been visiting friends in Mendocino, our favorite getaway destination on the northern California coast. While we were there, we stayed at our home base and made a point of relaxing, doing only what our hearts desired. We plugged in to the natural flow of each day and just let our minds drift as we enjoyed the beautiful environment. As we gave up our attachment to any agenda or timetable, we found magic in everything we did. One of the things we were inspired to do was to lay some flagstone in our patio area. The stones had been delivered earlier. The amount ordered was an educated guess that I had made the week prior. We got inspired and began laying the stones. We had a wonderful time watching each stone fit into its perfect place. At the end, it turned out that we had ordered the perfect amount of stones right down to the last one.

My husband and I had been delighting in the coincidences that were happening each day in Mendocino. We experienced small coincidences like our daughter calling exactly at the time when we could talk and our flagstone job finishing with exactly the right amount of material. Finally we headed home feeling relaxed and in the flow. We drove the back roads home (a change in pattern for us) in order to avoid traffic. We were on a familiar country road close to home when traffic suddenly slowed to an unusual crawl.

I looked ahead, only to see two horses running down the middle of the road with their saddles on but no riders! Cars in both directions were not stopping, but were slowing down and nudging the horses along, just keeping them moving in a direction. I'm sure the non-horse people's logic was to use their cars to pressure the horses into getting off the road so that the cars could resume driving at faster speeds. Someone familiar with horses would know immediately that this was a recipe for disaster.

Then the traffic stopped completely, so I jumped out of the car, knowing I had to help, especially as someone who knew about horses and their behaviors. As I ran past the crawling cars, I could see that a man had already caught one of the horses by the halter and was trotting with it in hand toward the other horse, still meandering free. I thought the second horse might feel as if it were being chased, so I yelled ahead to the man, suggesting he stop with the one horse and see if the second wouldn't come back to her buddy. He yelled back that he had already tried that and it had not worked. I knew that if he had already thought of that idea, he probably had some experience with horses and knew what might be a safe course of action, so I trusted that what he was doing was the right thing.

I caught up to him standing in the road with the one horse in hand. He proceeded to tell me that he knew these horses. They were boarders at his father's ranch just a few miles away. He said he was heading home and didn't usually come this way (a change in pattern for him) but was glad he had done so today. My next thought was, "I hope one of these mares does not belong to Genevieve." Genevieve was a teenage girl who was a friend of my daughter's and whose mother Donna was my friend. I knew that Genevieve used to board her horse at the stable this man had described as his father's facility. There were about 40 horses at this ranch. It was not likely that one of these horses would be Genevieve's.

We caught the second mare, who had not wandered too far away from her companion. Both horses seemed happy enough to be captured. I told the fellow that I too had a stable and could easily manage the two mares with my husband while he retrieved his car, which was blocking traffic. He moved his car, and then began a search for the missing riders. He and I were both concerned about their safety, given that saddled horses without riders is generally not a good sign. We also wondered how we could orchestrate getting the horses home. He decided to trust me with the horses as he headed off to find the riders.

My husband and I moved the horses onto a neighbor's property, just off the road, and were holding them when I noticed that the riders' helmets and bridles where still tied to the saddles. The horses were in their halters and the lead ropes were tied around their necks. In light of this, I realized the riders had not been thrown off; they must have been already off the horses, which had not been tied up securely. The horses had clearly escaped after the riders had dismounted. Realizing this brought us some relief because we knew the riders were probably not hurt. Then I said to my husband, "I sure hope one of these horses is not Genevieve's," but something inside me made me feel that one of them was. I didn't want to think of her having such a traumatic incident.

We had not been holding the horses for more than five minutes when Genevieve's mother, Donna, pulled up in her car. She jumped out looking anxiously at the horses and quickly recognized me. "Lisa and Richard," she exclaimed, "I can't believe this is you! Oh my God . . . this is amazing." She explained that she had received a call from her daughter saying that she and a girlfriend had ridden their horses several miles from the stables to a pond. They thought they'd take a quick dip to cool off on this warm day, so they put the halters on the horses and tied up the reins, figuring the horses would stay put and graze on the ample summer grass.

As soon as the girls dismounted and tied back the reins, the horses bolted! They took off running and left the girls far behind. Speaking with her mother on the phone, Genevieve was distressed and didn't know what to do. Her mother didn't know either, other than to pray that someone could safely catch the horses. She promptly left her work and set out to find both the horses and the girls.

When Donna arrived on the scene, it occurred to me that we were witnessing the true nature of *Ritam*, "accessing the conspiracy of improbabilities." The Universe had cleverly orchestrated the timing and travel not only of someone (the man on the street) who knew these horses and where they belonged, but also another couple of competent horse handlers (Richard and me) who also knew the owners, as well as the mother of the rider. What were the chances of these three parties arriving at that very spot at that very time, with no prior knowledge or preparation for this event?

Within another five minutes, the two girls walked up the road toward us and were reunited with their runaway horses. They had a teary reunion with their beloved mares and learned a few valuable lessons. All of us were filled with awe and wonder, impressed with the connectedness of all things, people, and events. Coincidences like those on that important day show us that at our core, we are all part of some sort of universal field that keeps us all connected and in relationship with each other.

That day, I saw and felt the confirmation that everything really is possible and that the core of our being is the ultimate shared reality. We can see evidence of this through coincidences in our lives that come in many forms. Our intentions really do have an infinite organizing power, and our willingness to bring our attention to these and other equally powerful aspects of awareness allows us to appreciate what it means to be *in the field*. This is true for everyone, though even more so for those of us who have the privilege of being *in the field, with horses.*

EPILOGUE

THE HORSE—a beautiful, powerful, sentient being—
provides an ongoing opportunity for humankind to consciously experience our own fields of energy and the dynamic interrelated power of Presence, Awareness, and
Intention. As you have seen in this book, thoughtful interactions with horses can reveal extraordinary levels of subtlety and energetic connection. I am certain we have only
just begun to scratch the surface of this wonder-filled *field of
connectivity* all life shares.

Perhaps you have had similar EquuSatori experiences
as those that I share in this book. If so, I invite you to come
to our *online field* where you can share your own EquuSatori
experiences and help us build a community. Even if you
have never been near a horse, come visit our online field to
read more EquuSatori stories submitted by others.

Also, feel free to invite others to *join the herd*. Tell those you know who will find this book of value to them about the EquuSatori community and invite them to visit the on-line site.

By sharing your personal EquuSatori with us all, you will extend the global opportunity we have for greater appreciation and understanding of horse-human relationships as they continue to emerge. Enjoy!

GO TO WWW.EQUUSATORI.COM TO SHARE
AND READ EQUUSATORI EXPERIENCES

ALSO FOLLOW LISA WALTERS ON TWITTER:
@LISAEQUUSATORI

ABOUT THE EQUUSATORI CENTER

⸻

THE EQUUSATORI CENTER, located in Sebastapol, CA. provides opportunities for individuals to engage in Equine Experiential Learning. In addition, Lisa teaches classical horsemanship and personalized skill-building for people who are interested in working in the Equine Experiential Learning fields.

A variety of programs for business and private groups are offered throughout the year and by request.

PLEASE VISIT WWW.EQUUSATORI.COM
FOR CURRENT INFORMATION AND PROGRAMS

Made in the USA
San Bernardino, CA
02 December 2015